GREAT NO-HIT GAMES OF THE MAJOR LEAGUES

Frank Graham, Jr. tells of the greatest moments of ten major league pitchers. Included are: Walter Johnson, Paul "Daffy" Dean, Johnny Vander Meer, Bob Feller, Allie Reynolds, Alva "Bobo" Holloman, Sal Maglie, Don Larsen, Bill Monbouquette and Sandy Koufax.

Great No-Hit Games of the Major Leagues

by **FRANK GRAHAM, JR.**

Illustrated with photographs

RANDOM HOUSE  **NEW YORK**

Grateful acknowledgement is made to Charles Scribner's Sons for permission to use an excerpt from "Horseshoes," from *Round Up* by Ring Lardner. Copyright by Charles Scribner's Sons, 1924.

Library of Congress Catalog Card Number: 68-14487

Manufactured in the United States of America

Little League Baseball is greatly pleased to join with Random House in the establishment of a Little League Library. It is our confident belief that the books thus provided will prove both entertaining and helpful for boys of Little League age and indeed for their parents and all who are Little Leaguers at heart.

This is one of a series of official Little League Library Books. Each has been read and approved at Little League Headquarters. We hope they will bring enjoyment and constructive values to all who may have the opportunity of reading them.

P J McGovern

President and Chairman of the Board
Little League Baseball, Incorporated

Contents

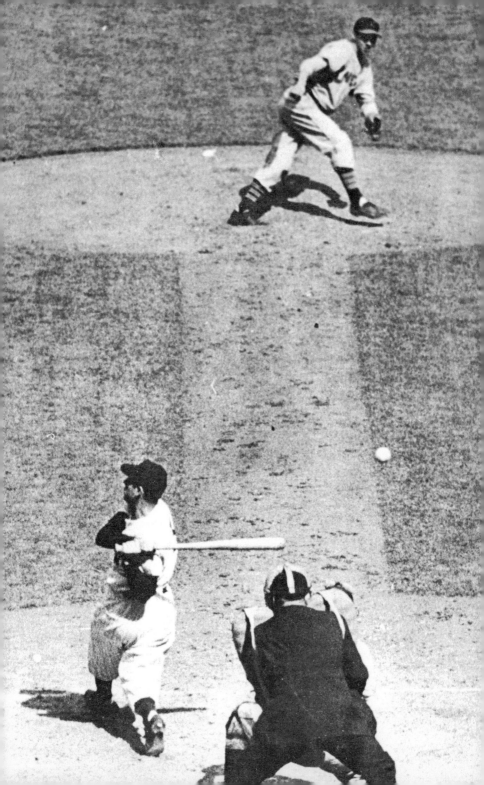

Introduction

When a pitcher goes to the mound, he tries to keep the other team from hitting. This is an essential part of baseball. The pitcher who is the most successful at this is usually the pitcher who wins the game. If he is *completely* successful, he pitches a no-hit game.

Naturally, no-hit games are very rare. Sometimes a whole season will go by without a no-hitter being pitched in the major leagues. When a man does pitch a no-hit game, he generally looks on it as his finest performance.

This book tells the story of some of the great no-hit games of the major leagues. Of course, there have been other outstanding games but there are not enough pages to include all of them. For example, there was the game that Harvey Haddix of the Pittsburgh Pirates pitched against the Milwaukee Braves in 1959. For 12 innings Haddix pitched a perfect game and did not allow a Milwaukee batter to reach first base. But *his* team was not hitting either. The score remained 0-0 until the 13th inning, when Haddix finally gave up a hit and lost the game, 1-0.

In 1965 there were the *two* games in which Jim

Maloney of the Cincinnati Reds pitched no-hit ball for ten innings. In the first of those games he was beaten, 1-0, in the eleventh inning, when the New York Mets got their only two hits. Later that year, Maloney won a ten-inning no-hitter against the Chicago Cubs, also by a score of 1-0.

And, of course, there was the no-hitter which Joel Horlen of the Chicago White Sox pitched against the Detroit Tigers in September, 1967, as his team battled for the American League pennant. It is always exciting to watch a no-hitter being pitched in the thick of a close pennant race.

But each of the games described in this book was something special. So were the men who pitched them.

GREAT NO-HIT GAMES OF THE MAJOR LEAGUES

1. The Big Train's Belated Arrival

Ring Lardner was a sports reporter before he became one of America's most famous short-story writers. From his baseball experiences he wrote a story about a rookie outfielder in the big leagues. In one of his first games, the unfortunate rookie batted against Walter Johnson, who was known as the best pitcher who ever lived. This is how the rookie in Ring Lardner's story described what happened:

> They can't never tell me Johnson throws them balls with his arm. He's got a gun concealed about his person and he shoots 'em up there. . . . So I just tried to meet the first one he throwed, but when I stuck out my bat Henry [the catcher] was throwing the pill back to Johnson.

With Walter Johnson on the mound the Senators were an exciting team.

Then I thought, maybe if I start swingin' now at the second one I'll hit the third one. So I let the second one come over and the ump guessed it was another strike, though I'll bet a thousand bucks he couldn't see it no more'n I could. While Johnson was still windin' up to pitch again I started to swing—and the big cuss crossed me with a slow one. I lunged at it twice and missed it both times, and the force of my wallop throwed me clean back to the bench. The Ath-a-letics was all laughin' at me and I laughed too, because I was glad that much of it was over.

In real life, not only the rookies of those days but also the great hitters told the same sort of story about Walter Johnson. In every generation, there is one pitcher who is more exciting than all the other pitchers of his time. In our day, that pitcher has been Sandy Koufax. In our fathers' day, Bob Feller attracted the most attention. And back in the early years of this century, when our grandfathers were young men, Walter Johnson was the most feared pitcher in baseball.

Johnson relied on his overpowering fast ball, which he threw with a side-arm motion. His curve ball was not as explosive as either Koufax's or Feller's. But his fast ball was so good that he won 416 games, more than any other pitcher in the history of the American League; and he struck out 3,497 batters, more than any other pitcher in the history of baseball!

"You knew you were going to get that fast ball every time you faced him," said Ty Cobb, one of baseball's greatest hitters. "You never had to guess. You could get set for the fast ball, but you still couldn't hit it. Walter was the fastest."

Billy Evans, a famous umpire of the time, had the best possible place from which to judge Johnson's fast ball when he called "balls" and "strikes" behind the plate. Evans agreed with Cobb.

"Johnson was the only pitcher who made me close my eyes instinctively as his pitch came at me," Evans said. "When I was umpiring behind the plate I tried to glue my eyes to every pitch, but his were too much for me. I remember once when Joe Gideon of the Yankees was at bat. The last time I saw it, this pitch of Johnson's looked like it was going to be a strike. So that's the way I called it.

"Gideon looked back at me, kind of blinking, and he asked, 'What was it, a fast ball or a curve?'

" 'Why ask me about it?' I said.

"Gideon shrugged and grinned. 'I never saw it. I had to close my eyes.'

"That made me feel better. I knew the ballplayers couldn't second-guess me if they were closing their eyes, too."

Everybody agreed that Johnson was the *best*. The only trouble was that he spent most of his career pitching for the Washington Senators, who, in those days, were just about the *worst*. There is a phrase that is often used to describe the achievements of the first American President: "George Washington—first in war and first in peace." With regard to the Senators, many people used to turn that saying into a joke: "Washington—first in war, first in peace, and last in the American League!"

No one can guess how many games Johnson might have won if he had been pitching for a pennant contender. Because he played with a poor team, he had to work hard for every victory. For example, he pitched in 59 games that were decided by a score of 1-0, and he won 40 of them. Many great athletes have gone down in history as "Good Joes," mainly because they were always with a winning team. In addition to being a great athlete, Walter Johnson possessed the strength of character to be a good loser.

One afternoon, in Boston, Johnson was involved in one of the extremely close games that had become typical of the Senators. When the Red Sox came to bat in the last half of the ninth inning, the score was still 0-0. Johnson got the first two batters out, but the next one reached base. The fourth man to come to bat in the inning hit the ball into center field. He should have been held to a single, but Clyde Milan, Washington's center fielder, let the ball roll between his legs. The runner scored all the way from first base and the Red Sox won, 1-0.

Afterward, Milan came over to Johnson in the

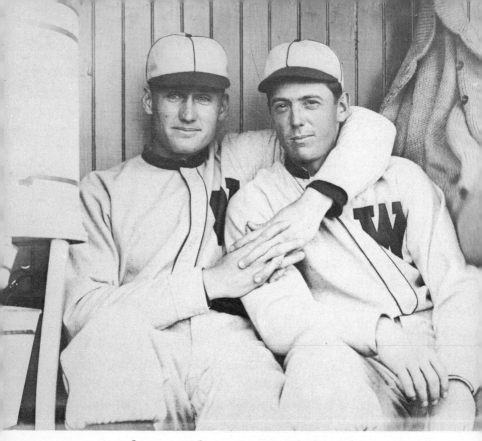

Johnson with teammate Clyde Milan.

clubhouse to apologize for losing the game. But
Johnson tried to cheer him up.

"That's all right, Clyde," he said. "You don't do
a thing like that very often. And besides, I should
have struck the batter out."

Life had never been easy for Johnson. He was born
on a small farm in Kansas on November 6, 1887.
The family was very poor, and later Walter's father
moved them to California. There, Walter grew into

a husky young man, standing 6-feet 2-inches tall and weighing over 200 pounds. He played baseball whenever he found the opportunity, and pretty soon the big league scouts heard about this nice-looking boy who could throw the ball harder than anybody else in the state.

Walter was signed by the Senators. He was a star from the very beginning. Whenever it was announced that Johnson was going to pitch, people would come to the ball park because, with Johnson on the mound, the Senators were an exciting team.

But Walter could not pitch every day of the week. On those days when he was on the bench, the Senators generally lost. For the first five years that Johnson was with the team, the Senators never finished higher than next-to-last place. Fans all over the country admired Johnson for the way he pitched his heart out for a losing team.

His admirers used to call him "The Big Train" because his fast balls seemed to come roaring in like an express train. Sometimes the fans and writers called him "Swede" because they believed that Johnson was a Swedish name. Once, when a friend of his found out that Johnson's parents were really Scotch-Irish, he asked him why he didn't correct the mistake.

"Oh, no, I wouldn't do that," Johnson said. "The Swedes are mighty fine people and I don't want to do anything that might offend them."

Johnson was as fine a man as he was a pitcher. He did not smoke or drink, he attended church regularly, and he extended his good will even to the opposing players. This meant that he refused to use his fast ball as a weapon. Another pitcher might have thrown at the batters to keep them terrified. But Johnson believed that winning a game was not important enough to risk injuring another man.

Some players took advantage of Johnson's good nature. One day, when Johnson was wild, he struck Eddie Collins of the White Sox on the leg. Collins fell to the ground and rolled around like a man in great pain. Johnson rushed in to see if he could help him, but Collins kept moaning and rubbing his leg. Finally, he climbed to his feet and limped down to first base.

Returning to the mound, Johnson was upset by the incident. He did not like to hurt a man. And, of course, with Collins a "cripple" on first base, Johnson did not watch him very closely, but concentrated instead on the batter. Suddenly, as he threw to the plate, Collins came to life and took off for second base, stealing the base easily. Then Collins dusted himself off and grinned, showing everybody in the ball park that he had tricked the great Walter Johnson.

Afterward, somebody asked Johnson if he was angry about being tricked by Collins.

Walter shook his head. "It was nice to know that Eddie wasn't really hurt," he said.

Yet no pitcher in baseball history tried harder to win than Johnson did. Pitching against Boston one day, he struck out *four* batters in one inning. This unlikely feat occurred because, when Johnson struck out the third batter, the Washington catcher could not hold onto the pitch. And while the catcher tried to recover the ball, the batter reached first base. Unruffled, Walter simply bore down and struck out the fourth man.

Johnson is shown in 1913, accepting a gift of an automobile.

On another occasion, when the Senators were short of pitchers, Johnson pitched three straight games against the Yankees. He won all three by shutouts!

"I felt like my arm was going to fall off, so I hid in the clubhouse before the fourth game," Johnson said later. "I didn't want the manager to get any more ideas like that."

And yet, as the years went by, the greatest thrill that a pitcher can have seemed to escape Johnson. He had never pitched a no-hit game. By 1920 he had been pitching in the American League for 14 seasons and his arm was not as strong as it had been in his earlier years.

On July 1 of that year, the Senators traveled to Boston for a series with the Red Sox. As usual, there was a certain amount of excitement in the stands when the great Johnson walked to the pitcher's mound. Harry Harper, who had once been Johnson's teammate at Washington, was on the mound for the Red Sox. Harper was only a fair pitcher, but anyone had a good chance against the weak-hitting Senators. The two pitchers dueled through the early innings, with neither of them giving up a run. For Johnson, it must have looked like the same old story—pitching his heart out, only to be beaten by his teammates' failure to score.

Then, in the seventh inning, the Senators broke through. Sam Rice, their young center fielder, slashed a single to center. Bob Roth's grounder forced Rice out at second base, but Hank Shanks kept the rally alive with a single to right field. Roth raced to third.

Harper, fearing that one run would probably decide this well-pitched game, worked carefully on the next batter and struck him out. With two out, Harper felt that he could breathe a little more easily, although there were Washington runners on first and third. The next batter was second baseman Bucky Harris.

Harper pitched just as carefully to Harris, but the Senators' second baseman hit the ball sharply back to the mound. Harper made a stab at the ball, but it bounced off his glove and over toward shortstop. By the time the shortstop could reach the ball, Harris was past first base and Roth had raced home with the first run of the ball game.

Now, with the scoreless tie broken and their team trailing, 1-0, the Boston fans noticed that this was no longer an ordinary ball game. Through the first six innings, Johnson had not allowed a Boston batter to reach base. In the bottom of the seventh inning, the Red Sox came to bat trying to start a rally of their own. Harry Hooper, the Red Sox' veteran outfielder, led off against Johnson. He hit an easy grounder near second base. Bucky Harris, who had just driven in the Senators' run with his infield hit, moved in front of the ball—and fumbled it! He groped for the ball, couldn't find it, and watched helplessly as Hooper reached first base.

But there was no question about this play. It should have been an easy out, and the official scorer correctly called it an error. The Red Sox had their first base runner of the game, but they still had not gotten a hit off Johnson. The Senators' great pitcher, working as calmly as ever, pitched his way out of the inning with no further damage.

At that point, even the Boston fans were rooting openly for Johnson to pitch the no-hitter he had been wanting for so long. Through the eighth inning, the excitement mounted as Johnson set down the Red Sox in one-two-three order. The Senators could not score in the top half of the ninth inning, and Johnson walked out to the mound in the last half, trying to preserve both his victory and his no-hit game.

The Red Sox were not going to serve him his no-hitter on a platter. They sent up Ben Karr to bat for the catcher. Johnson, proving his greatness as he had done so many times in the past, called on his fast ball just when he needed it the most. Karr waved feebly at three pitches and then walked back to the dugout, Johnson's ninth strikeout victim of the game.

Johnson turned to face the next batter, Hack Eibel, pinch hitting for Harper. Once more Johnson overpowered the batter. He threw his fast ball past

Eibel three times and he, too, trudged back to the dugout, Johnson's tenth strikeout victim.

The Boston fans knew that they were watching one of baseball's most dramatic moments. The prize was almost within the grasp of this aging pitcher. The last batter Johnson had to face was Hooper, a .300 hitter who was perhaps the most dangerous man in the Red Sox' line-up.

Johnson fired to the plate, and the heart of every fan in the park sank at the sharp crack of bat against ball. Hooper had "pulled" Johnson's pitch sharply toward right field. But Joe Judge, the Senators' first baseman, made a quick lunge to his right and speared the ball. Johnson raced off the mound toward first base, which Judge had left uncovered. Johnson, Hooper and the throw from Judge all seemed to arrive at the base at the same time. But Johnson reached for the ball and planted his foot on the bag a fraction of a second before Hooper came down on it.

When the umpire lifted his arm to signal that Hooper was out, it was as if he had pulled a switch, letting loose the cheers of the crowd. There was a roar of approval for a great pitching performance. The crowd was also paying a long-delayed tribute to a man whose finest moment had come after 14 years of wonderful pitching for a lost cause.

2. Dizzy's Kid Brother

Late in the summer of 1934, one of the most colorful teams baseball fans have ever seen came charging out of nowhere to make a bid for the National League pennant. The players' names are enough to excite the fans who remember them— Frankie Frisch, "The Fordham Flash" . . . Pepper Martin, "The Wild Hoss of the Osage" . . . Joe "Ducky-Wucky" Medwick . . . James "Ripper" Collins . . . Leo "The Lip" Durocher . . . Jerome "Dizzy" Dean and his kid brother, Paul "Daffy" Dean. These were the St. Louis Cardinals, but the newspapers of their time called them "The Gashouse Gang."

Members of the 1934 Gashouse Gang: left to right, Dizzy Dean, Leo Durocher, Ernie Orsatti, Bill

In June, the Cardinals were in sixth place in the National League. Their star pitcher, Dizzy Dean, who made no effort to conceal his contempt for the American League, said at the time: "If we were in that other league, we would win the pennant."

And the Cardinals' shortstop, Leo Durocher, who was standing nearby, replied: "They wouldn't let us in the other league. They would say we were a lot of gashouse ballplayers."

Durocher meant that the Cardinals were a fight-

DeLancey, Rip Collins, Joe Medwick, Frankie Frisch, John Rothrock and Pepper Martin.

ing bunch, who looked as if they had come right out of a rough-and-tumble neighborhood down by the railroad tracks, the waterworks or the gashouse. Their uniforms were always dirty from sliding into bases head-first. They picked fights with other teams and brawled among themselves. But they were good. And, above all, they had confidence in themselves.

Slowly, after July 4, they began to move up in the league standings. Frisch, their manager and second baseman, was one of the finest all-around players of his time. Medwick was a deadly right-handed hitter. Durocher was a fiery, fancy-fielding shortstop. But no team can win without good pitching, and in the Dean brothers the Cardinals had something special.

"Frisch is the greatest manager baseball's ever seen," Dizzy Dean told the sports writers. "He's the only man who could keep a team in a pennant fight with a two-man pitchin' staff."

Left to right: Paul Dean, Dizzy Dean and Frankie Frisch.

Diz, of course, was talking about himself and his kid brother. It was obvious to Cardinal fans that Dizzy believed he and Paul were the whole show. In most cases, however, nobody minded Dizzy when he bragged about himself. People scorn only the braggart who doesn't produce, and Dizzy Dean was producing victories for the Cardinals.

As nearly as anyone can determine, Jerome "Dizzy" Dean was born in Arkansas before World War I. His brother, Paul, was born a few years later. Their father was a migratory farm worker, and the family never settled in one place for very long.

"Once we was drivin' across the Southwest, me and Pa in one car, my uncle and my brother Paul in another car right behind us. We come to a railroad crossin' and there was a freight train headin' for it, too. Pa and me got across but Paul and my uncle didn't quite make it. It was a long train and, you know, we didn't see Paul and my uncle again for two years!"

If some of Dizzy's stories about his boyhood are hard to believe, at least he was telling the truth when he said the family moved too often for him to spend much time in school. "I didn't go to school but two years," he said. "If I'd gone another two years I'd have caught up to my Pa."

Somewhere along the way, a scout for the St. Louis Cardinals heard about Dizzy and his

strong right arm. According to Dizzy, the scout
came upon him as he was throwing stones at squirrels in the woods.

"I was throwin' those stones with my *left* hand,"
Dizzy said, "and when that scout found out I was
a right-hander he wanted to know how come I
was usin' my left. I just told him the truth. I said
that I threw so hard with my right hand that
I squashed up them squirrels somethin' terrible,
and they wasn't fit eatin' then."

Dizzy joined the Cardinals in 1932, and his loud
mouth and blazing fast ball made him a rookie sen-
sation. He won 18 games and led the league
in strikeouts that year. In 1933 he won 20 games
and was again the league's strikeout leader. In one
game he struck out 17 Chicago batters. In another
game he bunted for a "home run."

It wasn't really a home run, but the results were
the same. The Cardinals were playing the Giants.
When Dizzy came to bat with a runner on first
base, the Giants pulled their infield in, looking for
a bunt. Dizzy shortened up his bat to bunt and the
third baseman came charging in to field it. Dean,
however, gave the ball a little slap and it sailed
over the third baseman's head into left field. When
Dean saw that the left fielder was a little slow in
retrieving the ball, he kept right on running around
first base. The left fielder tried to cut him down at
second base, but his throw was wild and rolled all

After beating the Detroit Tigers, Dizzy acts out his feat in the clubhouse by twisting the tail of an inflated rubber tiger.

the way to the right field corner. Diz kept right on
running and scored standing up with what he
liked to call his "home run."

With every victory, Dizzy's voice grew louder.
He had a sense of humor, too. One afternoon, when
umpire George Barr called a close pitch against
him, Dizzy rushed in to argue the point.

"You mean to say that wasn't a strike?" Dizzy
shouted at the umpire.

Barr just shook his head and turned away. Dizzy
followed him.

"Mr. Barr, ain't you even goin' to answer my
question?"

"I did answer your question, young man," Barr
told him. "I shook my head."

"No, you didn't," Dizzy said. "If you had I'd have
heard somethin' rattle."

It was about this time that Dizzy's conversation
began to shift from himself to someone else. His
kid brother, Paul, became the subject most of the
time. He had to admit, Dizzy said, that no matter
how good he himself was, his kid brother was even
better. Dizzy could throw a baseball harder than
anybody else in the world—except Paul, who could
throw even harder. Dizzy finally talked the Cardinals into signing Paul.

Paul's career in the minor leagues had been brief.
He could, as Dizzy said, throw the ball very hard.
He pitched a no-hit game in 1932, when he was a

member of the Columbus Red Birds, a Cardinal
farm team. The next year he won 22 games and lost
only 7. He was just 21 years old at the time, but
the Cardinals thought he had enough "stuff" to become a winning pitcher in the National League. So
in 1934 they brought him up from the Red Birds to
join his brother.

Paul Dean was a quiet, unpretentious man. He
did not like to be around people, a trait that made
him the exact opposite of his famous brother. At
the ball park, Paul could usually be found sitting
alone somewhere, far from the jostling and kidding
of his Cardinal teammates. The more people left
him alone, the better he liked it.

Surprisingly, he wasn't even very enthusiastic
about baseball. "All baseball ever did for me was
ruin my cotton-pickin' career," he once said cyni-
cally.

Although he did not share his brother's great
enthusiasm for people and baseball, at least he admired the way Dizzy performed on the pitcher's
mound.

"I think all the other players on this club ought
to volunteer to take a cut in pay," Paul said. "That
way Diz can get the salary he wants."

Perhaps that was one reason why the other players gave Paul the name "Daffy." But they didn't
mind having the Dean brothers around, even though
they sometimes got sick of hearing Diz talk about

the wonderful feats of "me and Paul." The Dean boys were pitching the Cardinals into the thick of the pennant fight.

As the Cardinals moved in on the league leaders, there was a constant uproar in the clubhouse. Paul didn't say very much, but Dizzy said more than enough for both of them. When Diz believed that his kid brother wasn't getting enough money, *he* went on strike. Later in the season, Diz became so upset by one of Manager Frisch's orders that he tore his uniform into shreds. The Cardinals fined him, and also made him pay for the uniform. Diz paid the fine without any complaint, but he resented being billed for the uniform.

"They could have mended it," he grumbled.

The Cardinals were seven and a half games behind the Giants when they began their final long road trip of the season. If they were ever to win the pennant, they would have to make their move at this time. The Cardinals arrived in New York (where the Giants played their games in those days) for an important series. They relied, of course, on the Dean boys.

Daffy won the opening game of the series, shutting out the Giants in 12 innings, 2-0. Two days later, Dizzy beat them in the first game of a double-header, 5-3, and Daffy came back to win the second game, 3-1. The Gashouse Gang was closing in on the Giants.

On September 21, the Cardinals went to Brooklyn (where the Dodgers played in those days) for a double-header. The Cardinals had to win both games to pick up ground on the Giants, but the Dodgers, though they were in sixth place, could be pesky. Manager Frisch, as usual, called on his two best pitchers. Before the season had begun, Dizzy had boasted that "Me and Paul will win 45 games between us." If each of them won on this day in Brooklyn, Dizzy's boast would become a reality—Dizzy had already won 26 games, and Daffy had won 17.

More than 18,000 fans were in Ebbets Field as Dizzy strutted out to the mound to pitch the first game. It was an easy one for him. Ripper Collins, the Cardinals' first baseman, drove in six runs to help build a 13-0 lead over the Dodgers. Dizzy did not give up a base hit until the eighth inning. Then Ralph Boyle of the Dodgers beat out an infield roller for the first hit. Dizzy, secure behind his 13-0 lead, relaxed a little in the ninth inning and gave the Dodgers two more harmless singles before he got the last out.

It was Daffy's turn in the second game. No one, of course, expected him to come close to Dizzy's splendid three-hit shutout in the first game. Paul did not get the batting support that the Cardinals had given Dizzy, but his teammates made some fine fielding plays. In the first inning, Lonnie Frey of the Dodgers slashed what looked like a sure base hit into left center-field. Joe "Ducky-Wucky" Medwick, however, raced into the hole to make a running catch. A few innings later, Medwick ran back to make a one-handed, leaping catch of a long drive by Sam Leslie to the base of the left field wall.

Meanwhile, Ray Benge of the Dodgers was matching Paul pitch for pitch. The score was still 0-0 when the Cardinals came to bat in the sixth inning. Then Paul himself scored what proved to be

Paul "Daffy" Dean on the mound.

the winning run. He led off by walloping a double to left center-field. A moment later Ripper Collins, the batting star of the first game, drove Paul home with a sharp single to right.

The fans in Ebbets Field began to realize that the Dodgers' only base runner of the game had been Len Koenecke, who had walked in the first inning. Brooklyn had not gotten a single hit off Paul. Throwing harder in the late innings, Dean set down the Dodgers in the seventh, then struck out two of the three batters who faced him in the eighth.

Meanwhile, his teammates were pecking away at Benge. Medwick doubled and scored in the seventh inning, and in the ninth he tripled and scored on a grounder by Collins. As Daffy walked out to pitch the last half of the ninth inning, he held a 3-0 lead.

Brooklyn fans were never noted for their love for visiting players. Yet now, as Daffy struggled to protect his no-hit game, the fans began to root for him. Even in Brooklyn, where *everything* was supposed to happen in those days, the fans seldom had a chance to see a no-hitter, and they were eager for Daffy to finish the job.

The Dodgers' manager was Casey Stengel, who later became famous as the manager of the Yankees and the Mets. Casey wanted to break up Daffy's no-hitter and perhaps save the game for his team. He sent left-hander Jimmy Bucher up to pinch hit for catcher Al Lopez.

Daffy threw a fast ball and Bucher swung and missed. Daffy got his next pitch over the outside corner of the plate for strike two. He was not wasting any pitches now. He came right back with another pitch over the outside corner, and Bucher watched it go past. When the umpire called him out on strikes, the crowd sent up a mighty cheer.

Next, it was pitcher Benge's turn to bat, but Stengel looked down his bench and chose another left-handed pinch hitter. This time, it was Johnny McCarthy. Daffy wound up and fired a fast ball. McCarthy swung and hit a high pop fly, which Manager Frisch called for and caught near second base. There were two out, and the crowd urged Daffy to retire the last batter.

This batter was Ralph "Buzz" Boyle, the Dodgers' right fielder, whose slow roller in the first game had ruined Dizzy's bid for a no-hitter. Daffy kept the ball low, and Boyle hit it on the ground toward shortstop. Leo Durocher, then one of the surest fielders in baseball, moved swiftly in front of the ball, but it took a twisting, short hop into his glove and then popped right out. Leo pounced on the loose ball, picked it up and fired to Collins at first base. Umpire Ziggy Sears' hand went up in the signal for "out," and Daffy Dean had his no-hit game.

The Brooklyn fans poured out of the stands onto

the field to congratulate him. But Dizzy, bounding from the Cardinals' dugout, was the first to reach him. He threw his arm around his kid brother and escorted him off the field as the fans milled around and slapped them on the back.

In the clubhouse a few minutes later, Dizzy strutted up and down in front of the lockers, telling everybody what a great pitcher his brother, Paul, was. The Cardinals were rolling now, and a few days later they would overtake the Giants and clinch the pennant. But meanwhile, Dizzy had only one complaint to make about his brother's wonderful performance.

"I wish I'd known you was goin' to pitch a no-hitter," he said to Paul. "Then I'd have bore down in the first game and got *me* one, too."

Curiously enough, Daffy, who never became a great pitcher, was the only one of the Dean boys to pitch a no-hitter. Dizzy, one of baseball's greatest pitchers, never again came close to pitching one. A no-hit game does not come easily to a pitcher—even a Dizzy Dean.

3. Two of a Kind

It was a sleepy afternoon in Cincinnati on June 11, 1938, and a small crowd had gathered at the ball park to watch the Reds play the Boston Bees. Around town there was an unusual amount of interest in the Reds that year. For a long time they had been a losing team, but they had finally gathered together some good young ballplayers, and it was thought that within a year or two they would win the pennant.

But, to most fans, that pennant was still in the future. For the moment, they were interested in watching one of the Reds' promising youngsters pitch against the Bees. He was a 23-year-old left-hander named Johnny Vander Meer. Johnny could throw the ball as hard as any other young pitcher in the league. And when he got his fast ball over the plate, he was very hard to beat. But on some days he was terribly wild, and on those occasions he didn't stay on the mound very long.

The Cincinnati fans were hoping that Vander Meer would pitch as well as he had the week before, in a game against the Giants. On that day, Johnny had beaten the Giants, 4-1, holding them to three hits. His fast ball had been "alive," as the ballplayers say, and he had had it under control.

Against the Bees, his fast ball seemed alive once more. He set down the first nine batters he faced. His opposing pitcher, "Deacon" Danny MacFayden, a cunning veteran, was pitching almost as well, and by the time the fourth inning began there was still no score.

For a moment it looked as if Vander Meer might have some trouble. He walked the first batter, Gene Moore. Then Johnny Cooney, the Bees' first baseman, hit a high pop fly back near the screen behind home plate. Big Ernie Lombardi, called "Schnozz" by his teammates because of his enormous nose, lumbered back and grabbed the foul. "Schnozz," for all his size, was an alert catcher. When he noticed that Moore had wandered off first base, he made a snap throw to catch him off the base and take Vander Meer out of trouble.

Left to right: Cincinnati manager Bill McKechnie, Johnny Vander Meer and catcher Ernie Lombardi.

The Reds gave Vander Meer the lead in their half of the fourth, when Wally Berger tripled and scored moments later on a sacrifice fly. But Vander Meer got right back into trouble in the fifth inning by walking the lead-off batter, Tony Cuccinello. Once more Lombardi took Vander Meer out of trouble with a quick throw, which trapped Cuccinello off base. With two out, Vander Meer gave up his third walk, but settled matters himself by getting Johnny Riddle to tap an easy ground ball back to the pitcher's mound.

In the last half of the fifth inning, Berger, who was the Reds' power hitter, gave Vander Meer a 3-0 lead by slamming a long home run with Lombardi on base. Then, as the sleepy crowd stirred with excitement, Vander Meer took complete charge of the game. The Bees' hitters were helpless in the face of his exploding fast ball.

In fact, Vander Meer made everything look very simple. Before anybody quite realized what had happened, Vander Meer had snuffed out the last Bee in the ninth inning. He walked off the field with the first no-hitter to be pitched in the National League since the day in 1934 when Daffy Dean had beaten the Dodgers in Brooklyn.

"Gee, I had no idea of pitching a no-hitter," said Johnny, stunned but very pleased, as he talked with the sportswriters in the clubhouse. "My arm felt better all the time as I went along. In the late innings I just kept bearing down harder and harder."

The news from Cincinnati was flashed across the country. A no-hit game is always important baseball news, and people wanted to know more about this handsome, dark-haired young man who had pitched a no-hitter in his first full season in the major leagues. Who *was* he?

Johnny Vander Meer had grown up in Midland Park, New Jersey. There his father, who had im-

migrated to the United States from Holland some
years before, worked as a stone mason. As a child,
Johnny had nearly died from an attack of appen-
dicitis. But as he regained his strength, he got out
onto the playing fields with the other boys, and
pretty soon he was known around town as a good
sandlot first baseman.

One day his team needed a pitcher. Johnny
threw left-handed, and the other fellows thought
that anybody who was left-handed would make a
good pitcher, so he was elected for the job.

"I didn't give up many hits, that's for sure,"
Johnny recalled some years later. "I just walked
everybody. I think I walked ten batters in less than
three innings, and finally they took me out and sent
me back to first base."

But every once in a while, Johnny made another
attempt at pitching. When he got his fast ball over
the plate, the other kids couldn't hit it. And although he continued to walk a lot of batters, he
pitched at least five sandlot no-hitters. On the
basis of his fast ball, he was signed to a contract
by the Dodgers.

For a long time it seemed that Johnny's career
would be cut short by his wildness. He simply
couldn't get the ball over the plate. He pitched for
several Dodger farm teams in the lower minor
leagues, but after a while the Dodgers let him go.
Later, the Boston Bees picked him up, and they

too gave up on him. Finally the Reds signed him.

But for a while, it was the same old story. Johnny couldn't get the ball over the plate. He was so discouraged that he thought about quitting baseball. Then, in 1936, he had a good season at Durham, North Carolina, winning 19 games, losing six and compiling a record of 295 strikeouts. In one game, he struck out 20 batters.

The Reds brought him to spring training in 1937, but they took one look at him and shipped him off to Syracuse, New York, so he could get more experience. And once again, Johnny was wild. He had a poor season, winning only five games and losing 11. For the second time, he thought about quitting baseball.

Then, in the spring of 1938, the Reds' manager, Bill McKechnie, went to work on him. McKechnie had been known for a long time as a skilled teacher of the art of pitching. Before coming to Cincinnati, he had worked wonders at Boston, taking castoff pitchers and turning them into winners.

McKechnie talked to Vander Meer about his pitching motion. One day the Reds were to play an exhibition game against the Boston Red Sox. McKechnie took Johnny aside.

"For a couple of weeks now I've been telling you how to hold the ball in front of you when you're winding up," McKechnie said. "Now today I want you to *watch*."

McKechnie pointed across the field to where
Lefty Grove, the Red Sox' great left-handed
pitcher, was warming up. Johnny watched him
for a while. Then he went over and introduced himself to Grove. The veteran left-hander was happy
to talk to the young man and give him some advice
on how to hold the ball before delivering it.

Afterwards, Johnny went back to McKechnie
and worked on what he had learned. By the time
the season opened, Vander Meer was getting the
ball over the plate more regularly. He was chosen
by McKechnie as one of the Reds' starting
pitchers.

Having justified McKechnie's faith in him by
pitching a no-hitter, Vander Meer found himself a
nationally acclaimed sports figure. He had scarcely
gotten used to the idea of being a star when he
learned that, only four days after pitching his no-
hitter, he was to take part in another historic event.

In 1938, night baseball was very unusual in the
major leagues. The first night game in the majors
had been played at Cincinnati in 1935. On that occasion, President Franklin D. Roosevelt had pushed
a button in the White House in Washington to turn
on the lights at the Reds' ball park. Three years
later, lights had been installed at Ebbets Field in
Brooklyn, and McKechnie told Vander Meer that
he would pitch there on June 15. It would be the

In the first night game played at Ebbets Field,
Vander Meer pitched before a crowd of 38,748 fans.

first major-league night game ever played in the
New York City area.

Johnny was understandably nervous. His family,
his girl friend and a lot of his buddies from New
Jersey were coming to Ebbets Field that night to
watch him pitch against the Dodgers.

"I wish Mom wasn't going to be here tonight,"
Johnny told a friend before the game. "When a fellow pitches a no-hitter, he usually doesn't do very
well his next time out. I don't want her to have to
sit there and watch me get bombed."

It was a thrilling evening at Ebbets Field. The
weather was perfect for baseball. A standing-
room-only crowd of 38,748 people packed the
stands, and among them was the great Babe Ruth.
There were special ceremonies before the game
began. An American Legion band marched out to
the flagpole and lowered the flag just before sun-
down. Jesse Owens, America's Olympic hero of two
years before, was on hand to give an exhibition.
He ran races against some of the faster ballplayers
(giving them a head start), and broad-jumped into
a special pit constructed in foul territory.

Vander Meer felt better once the game began.
The fans were curious to see how he would per-
form so soon after his no-hitter. Although no one
in baseball history had ever pitched two no-hit
games in a row, or even two in a season, the words
"no-hitter" were on a lot of people's lips. Certainly

they were on Johnny's mind as he faced the Dodgers that evening.

"I was trying for it all the way," he said afterward. "From the first batter on I bore down hard. I wanted only strikeouts."

Much of the pressure on Johnny was eased in the third inning, when the Reds scored four runs against the Dodgers' pitcher, Max Butcher. Three

First baseman Frank McCormick crosses the plate after hitting a three-run homer in the third inning.

of the four runs were scored on a homer by first baseman Frank McCormick. When Johnny came to bat in the sixth inning, the Dodgers still had not gotten a hit off him and the crowd gave him an ovation. He responded by dropping a bunt down the third-base line and beating it out for a hit. The crowd cheered even louder.

Vander Meer was sometimes wild, but even when he walked a man, the Dodgers could not get any hits to drive their runner around the bases. They were being overpowered by the hard-throwing left-hander. Trying to get a rally started in the sixth inning, the Dodgers sent up Gibby Brack as a pinch hitter. Vander Meer threw three fast balls past him to chalk up another strikeout.

Meanwhile, the Reds continued their assault on Brooklyn's pitchers. They scored a run in the seventh inning on a single by Harry Craft. In the eighth inning, Vander Meer came to bat with the cheers of the crowd ringing in his ears. Reaching first base as the result of a force-out at second, he scored a moment later on Wally Berger's booming triple, and the Reds led, 6-0.

The tension continued to mount in the last half of the eighth inning. Vander Meer was working on the impossible—a second straight no-hit game! He was wild, having already walked five batters, but the Dodgers could not touch his fast ball when he got it over the plate. Another pinch hitter,

Woody English, went down on strikes as Vander Meer breezed through the eighth inning.

"I was sitting in the stands near third base," Vander Meer's mother said later, "but I couldn't watch the last two innings. I turned my head away and prayed all the Dodgers would strike out."

As Vander Meer walked out of the dugout to pitch the last half of the ninth inning, the big crowd sent up a cheer that must have awakened babies all over Brooklyn. Certainly every adult in Brooklyn who was not at the ball park had his ear close to a radio as Vander Meer settled down to try for the last three outs that would make baseball history.

The first batter was Buddy Hassett, the Dodgers' left fielder. Johnny was trying hard now, perhaps too hard. He got two quick strikes across on Hassett, then threw three wide pitches. His next pitch was over the plate and Hassett hit a dribbler between the mound and first base. Vander Meer rushed to his left, picked up the ball, and tagged Hassett as he raced past. One out.

Then Vander Meer seemed to go to pieces. He walked catcher Babe Phelps. Cookie Lavagetto, the Dodgers' third baseman, was the next batter, and Vander Meer walked him, too. Now Dolf Camilli, the Dodgers' home-run-hitting first baseman, was at the plate. Johnny went from bad to worse— each pitch was wilder than the last. The crowd groaned as he threw four wild pitches to Camilli and walked him. The Dodgers had loaded the bases.

Then Manager McKechnie jumped off the Reds' bench and rushed out to the mound. "Settle down, Johnny," he told his pitcher. "Just pour that ball. They're more afraid than you are. Just pour that ball down their throats!"

The talk and the brief rest seemed to have an effect on Vander Meer. With new confidence, he went to work on the next batter, Ernie Koy. He

Excited teammates escort Vander Meer off the field after he has pitched his second no-hit game in a row.

got his first pitch over the plate and the crowd sent up a cheer. His next pitch was over, too, and Koy hit it on the ground down to third base. Lew Riggs did not take a chance on trying to start a double play with the speedy Koy running toward first base. Instead, he threw to the plate and cut off the run that would have ruined Johnny's shutout.

Now there were two out. Johnny's no-hitter was still intact, but the bases were still loaded. Only Leo Durocher, a great clutch ballplayer who had been the shortstop on the Gashouse Gang and was now the Dodgers' shortstop, stood between Vander Meer and his history-making performance.

Vander Meer swept low into his loose windup, resembling a *salaam*, which McKechnie had taught him during the spring. As the crowd held its breath, he reared back and fired to the plate. Durocher, swinging, got a piece of the ball, but it went high in the air toward short center-field. Harry Craft rushed in, waving everyone else away. The ball came down and settled in his glove, and the ball park shook under the cheers that went up for Vander Meer.

Johnny Vander Meer remains the only player in baseball history to have pitched consecutive no-hit games. His feat is one of the most remarkable in the record books and whenever his name is mentioned, it is usually even longer than it was originally—Johnny "Double No-Hit" Vander Meer!

4. A Great Pitcher Comes of Age

Perhaps the story of Bob Feller can best be told through his no-hit games. He was the third pitcher in the history of baseball to pitch three no-hit games during his career. Of Feller's three no-hitters, his last was the source of greatest pleasure to baseball men, fans and sports writers. This was not because Bob was a greater pitcher at the time or because he pitched a greater game. People were pleased because the hero, at last, had become a likeable human being.

No young player has ever been born with more talent than Bob Feller, nor has one become a suc-

Bob Feller as a 17-year-old big leaguer.

cessful big leaguer more quickly. He was born on a farm in Van Meter, Iowa. Bob's father hoped that his son would someday become a baseball star, and he practiced with him whenever he had a moment away from his chores.

For hours at a time, father and son would throw a baseball to each other. Even when Bob was a young boy, his father could see that he had a marvelous throwing arm. When Bob began pitching on local teams, none of the other boys could get their bats around in time to hit the ball. Word of his blazing fast ball spread quickly. When he was only 17 years old, the Cleveland Indians signed him. He reported directly to the Indians, without spending even a day in the minor leagues.

Feller, the 17-year-old big leaguer, was very wild, of course. But he threw his fast ball and his curve ball past the big-league hitters just as he had thrown it past his schoolmates back in Van Meter. In his second start he walked nine batters, but he set a new American League record by striking out 17! Bob Feller was making headlines at an age when most boys are trying to make their high school teams.

Feller got better every year. He was the most exciting pitcher in baseball. The crowds flocked to the ball park when "Rapid Robert" was pitching, hoping to see him pile up new strikeout records. He was so fast that somebody said he could "throw a lamb chop past a wolf." Yet many of the batters said his curve ball was even more difficult to hit than his fast ball. In the last game of the 1938 season, Feller broke his own record by striking out 18 batters.

In 1939 Bob won 24 games. When the 1940 season began, he was in a class by himself. He was named by the Indians' manager to pitch against the White Sox on opening day. Bob was blazing fast that April afternoon. He cut down the Chicago batters one by one, and when the game was over, Rapid Robert had become the first man ever to pitch a no-hit game on the first day of the season.

He was at the peak of his career. And yet the fans did not warm up to him as they had to Walter Johnson, Dizzy Dean, Babe Ruth and many of baseball's other superstars. Whether or not the fans and writers were right, many of them believed that Feller was "cold." They said that he was concerned more about making money for himself than winning a pennant for the Indians.

During 1940 an unfortunate incident occurred, convincing many people that the unpleasant stories about Feller were true. The Indians, who had not won a pennant since 1920, were battling the Yankees and the Tigers for the flag. Then, late in the season, a number of the Cleveland players, including Feller, asked the team's owner to fire their manager. They said he was too strict with them.

The story was printed in the newspapers. The sports writers and the players on the other teams made a big fuss about it. They called the Indians "The Cleveland Crybabies." Feller wasn't the only player who had complained, but he was the most famous, so he received most of the blame.

Bob won 27 games that season, and the Indians stayed in the pennant race until the very end. But, in his last game, Feller was beaten by Floyd Giebell, a rookie Tiger pitcher who had never before won a game in the major leagues. Detroit won the pennant. All over the country, fans were happy to learn that Feller and the rest of the "crybabies" had lost.

A year later, the United States entered World War Two. Many of the most famous athletes in the country waited to be drafted; or else they waited to see how the war would progress before enlisting. But Bob Feller became the first baseball star to volunteer for our country's armed services.

Feller joined the Navy, where he was made an athletic instructor. It was an easy job, and he probably could have spent most of the war in this country, just as other famous athletes did. But Feller wanted no special privileges. Other American boys were fighting in Europe and Asia. He saw no reason why he should stay behind in the United States, throwing a baseball and teaching boys to do push-ups, while there was a war going on.

Feller as the captain of a 40-millimeter gun crew aboard the battleship Alabama.

Feller completed a gunnery course. Then he began to pester his superior officers for a transfer to active duty. At last he got his wish. He was put in charge of a gun crew on the battleship *Alabama*. He saw action against Nazi U-boats in the North Atlantic. Later the *Alabama* moved to the Pacific, where Feller's gun crew shot down an enemy plane. His ship also took part in the liberation of the Philippine Islands. By the time the war was over, Feller had earned eight battle stars.

No one had served his country more unselfishly than Feller. At the peak of his career, he had given four years to the Navy, which may have cost him a chance to break many more pitching records. Yet, in spite of his sacrifice, Feller failed to become as popular with the fans as many less patriotic players who did not have his skills.

The year 1946 was an exciting one in the big leagues. After experiencing four seasons of below-standard "wartime" baseball, the fans saw the stars return to their teams. Naturally, it was an important event when, on April 30 of that year, Feller came to New York to pitch against the mighty Yankees.

In their line-up, the Yankees had many of baseball's most feared sluggers—Joe DiMaggio, Charley Keller, Tommy Henrich and Joe Gordon. No one had pitched a no-hitter against the Yankees in over 25 years.

More than 37,000 people came to Yankee Stadium on a weekday afternoon to see the game. Feller was wild at the start, walking one batter in each of the first four innings, and another one in the sixth. But he was blazing fast, just as he had been before the war. He fanned nine batters in the first five innings.

Floyd Bevens, who had a history of being a hard-luck pitcher, was opposing Feller for the Yankees. Although the Indians got an occasional hit off

Bevens, they could not score. Each inning, Yankee fans called on their team to get a rally started. But, each inning, Feller turned the Yanks back. By the eighth, the excitement that always goes with a no-hit game began to fill the big ball park.

Feller retired the Yankees' first two batters in the eighth inning. Everyone was tense now, the players as well as the fans. Phil Rizzuto, the Yankees' little shortstop, came to bat. He hit a high pop foul near third base. Ken Keltner, the Indians' veteran third baseman, settled under it for what should have been an easy catch, but the ball dropped out of his sweating hands.

Lou Boudreau, the Indians' manager as well as their shortstop, took the ball back to the dejected Feller.

"Tough break, Bob," he said to him. "But do this for me. Throw one more pitch to this fellow, as hard as you can. We'll get him."

Boudreau trotted back to his position, and Feller pitched once more to Rizzuto. The pitch was a little too good, however, and Rizzuto rapped it sharply on the ground past Keltner at third base. Keltner, diving desperately to atone for his error, could not touch the hard-hit ball. But Boudreau, rushing deep into the "alley" between third and short, made a brilliant backhanded stop, straightened up and made the long throw to first base for the out. Even Yankee fans were impressed by such a dramatic play, and they cheered as Feller and Boudreau went back to the dugout.

The score was still 0-0 when the Indians came to bat in the ninth inning. Then Frankie Hayes, Feller's catcher, took matters into his own hands. He pounded one of Bevens' fast balls into the lower left-field stands for a home run. As far back as anyone could remember, it was the first time a visiting player had received a rousing cheer for hitting a homer at Yankee Stadium. The Indians led, 1-0, and Feller had a chance to wrap up his no-hitter in the last half of the ninth.

George "Snuffy" Stirnweiss led off for the Yankees. On Feller's first pitch he faked a bunt. When Feller pitched again, Snuffy bunted along the first base line. Les Fleming, the Indians' first baseman, came in to field the ball—and fumbled it! It seemed that Feller's chance to pitch another no-hitter would be destroyed by the nervousness of his own teammates.

Stirnweiss was safe at first on the error. Tommy Henrich, the next batter, also bunted, sacrificing himself and allowing Stirnweiss to reach second. The Yankees' two best hitters, Joe DiMaggio and Charley Keller, were coming to bat. With the tying run on second base, Feller found that he was in danger of losing not only his no-hitter but the game itself.

It was a tense moment. DiMaggio, baseball's

During his second no-hit game Feller pitches to DiMaggio.

finest clutch hitter, faced Feller, baseball's finest clutch pitcher. Feller threw his famous curve, and DiMaggio hit the ball on the ground to Boudreau. He was thrown out, while Stirnweiss raced to third base.

Now there were two out and Keller came to bat. Keller, a broad-shouldered, scowling slugger, was called "King Kong" by his teammates because of his great strength. The bat looked like a toothpick in his hairy, muscular arms. Feller put two strikes across on Keller, but his next pitch was wide, for a ball. Stirnweiss was running up and down the third base line, faking a steal of home in the hope that Feller would become nervous and make a wild pitch.

But Feller, so close to his no-hitter, could not be rattled. He pitched again to Keller, and the Yankees' slugger hit the ball on the ground toward Ray Mack at second base. Mack, in his anxiety, stumbled and almost fell. Then he regained his balance, fielded the ball, and threw out the speeding Keller.

Rapid Robert had pitched a no-hitter against the most famous line-up of the time. It was truly one of the great no-hit games of the major leagues. He went on that year to win 26 games, and his 348 strikeouts that season set a modern record. But, in spite of Feller's greatness as a pitcher, the fans and players continued to feel that he was concerned only about himself.

By 1948 an arm injury had robbed Feller of his blinding fast ball. But he quickly developed an effective slider, which kept him up among the top stars in the game. That year, as the Indians rushed toward their first pennant since 1920, another unfortunate incident occurred, which revived many people's dislike for Feller.

In the middle of each season, an All-Star Game is played between the finest players in the American and National Leagues. Most of the players consider it an honor to be chosen to play, and the profits from the game are used to help retired ballplayers. But, for the second year in a row, Feller refused to play in the game. He claimed that he was tired.

The press severely criticized him for refusing. He was baseball's highest-paid pitcher, and most people felt that, because he was rich, he did not care what happened to the other players. Nearly every player in baseball was angry at Feller, and some said that he should be punished. Dixie Walker, who was a leader among the ballplayers, said:

"I can't understand how any player selected for an All-Star Game can fail to look on his selection as an honor. After all, it's the players' game, and if we don't do our best for it, we don't deserve to have it."

Pitching against the Boston Braves in the World Series that year, Feller learned how the fans felt

about him. He lost the first game that he pitched,
1-0. But the Indians came back and took the lead.
They needed only one more victory to clinch the
Series, and Feller was chosen to pitch against the
Braves at Cleveland. Almost 85,000 people were
in the stands that day, and they saw the Braves
knock Feller out of the box and win the game. As
Bob trudged back to the dugout, the boos and hoots
of the crowd began to rise. By the time he disappeared, the noise was deafening.

*Feller walks back to the dugout after being
knocked out of the box in the fifth game of the
1948 World Series.*

Although the Indians went on to win the Series, it was a great shock to this marvelous pitcher to learn how much the fans disliked him. But the incident taught him an important lesson. During the last years of his career, his surly behavior changed and he became one of the best-liked players on his team. He was no longer a *great* pitcher, but he was becoming a likeable human being.

An example of his new attitude toward his team occurred in 1950, just after he had been badly burned in a whirlpool bath. The Indians needed someone to pitch an important game. Feller, despite his pain, said that he would pitch.

"Wrapped in yards of cotton," the newspapers said the next day, "Bob not only won but pitched one of his best games."

George "Birdie" Tebbetts, a former catcher who had become a manager, was surprised at the change in Feller.

"I've been in baseball a long time," Tebbetts said, "but I've never seen anything to match this display of courage."

"The team needed me," Feller said. "It hadn't been going very well and I've been winning games. I just thought I could help."

Feller's new team spirit also showed in his efforts to help the country's young players. He became interested in Little League Baseball, and made sure that his sons played in the program.

Feller himself became the president of the League. Later on, he felt so strongly about the program's benefits that he wrote an article about Little League Baseball for *Sport* Magazine. He said, in part:

> Little League baseball can be a family adventure, that is, something which is shared by every member of the family. There are too few activities today in which the family can take part as a unit. I know that in our league the fathers serve as managers, umpires and groundskeepers. I even take a turn at umpiring if there is an emergency, although it's a job that's too tough for my liking. The mothers and sisters in the neighborhood serve as score-keepers or help out with registration. And, of course, everybody comes out and roots during the games. We *all* have fun.

In the first game of a double-header on July 1, 1951, Feller walked to the mound to pitch against the Detroit Tigers. His great fast ball was only a memory now, but he still had courage and skill. On this day, Feller was once more an unbeatable pitcher. His performance was not dramatic. He did not strike out the batters as he had during his first no-hitter. He did not face a line-up of superstars as he had during his second no-hitter. His pitching seemed as simple as a leisurely walk on a quiet day.

Using his curve ball and his slider, he smothered the Tigers. When he got the last out in the ninth inning, Feller walked off the mound with the third

After methodically pitching his third no-hitter, Feller receives the excited congratulations of catcher Jim Hegan.

no-hit game of his career. Only two old-timers, back in the early days of the major leagues, had ever pitched three no-hit games in their careers.

The fans set up a heart-warming cheer as Feller disappeared into the dugout. Their cheers were only a reflection of the way fans all over the country now felt about him. They had no doubt that Feller was a great pitcher. But, even more important, they liked him as a man, too.

5. The Super Chief

Anyone looking up the name Allie Reynolds in the record books would not find it in many places. Reynolds did not win as many games as most of the other pitching greats. He did not pile up exciting strikeout totals; and he seldom won any awards. But he was known as Casey Stengel's "clutch" pitcher. During Stengel's early years as the Yankees' manager, whenever the team had to play an important game, Stengel usually counted on his big part-Indian pitcher from Oklahoma, Allie Reynolds.

The 1950's were exciting years at Yankee Stadium. Some of the Yankees' most reliable players —Tommy Henrich and Charley Keller, for example—had already retired. But there were other outstanding players to take their places—Mickey Mantle, Yogi Berra, Billy Martin and Hank Bauer. The Yankees won the pennant almost every year.

But no team, no matter how famous its players or how many home runs it hits, can win consistently unless it has at least a couple of good pitchers. The pitcher is the most important player on the team. The Yankee teams of the 1950s had solid pitching staffs, and their "ace" was Reynolds.

Joe DiMaggio himself had suggested that the Yankees make a trade for Reynolds. Allie, who had Creek Indian blood in his veins, had lived so far out in "the wilds" that he had never played baseball before entering college. In fact, at Oklahoma A. & M. he was better known as a football player. In 1942, after a couple of seasons in the minor leagues, he joined the Cleveland Indians.

Allie always could throw hard, but he had much to learn about the art of pitching. By 1943 he was becoming one of the better pitchers in the American League. He led the league in strikeouts that year. In 1945 he won 18 games, but led the league in bases on balls.

Reynolds was what is commonly known as a "late bloomer." He once told a friend, "My son had pitched more games by the time he finished playing Little League ball than I had pitched by the time I reached the big leagues."

When Reynolds slumped in 1946, winning only 11 games and losing 15, many baseball men believed that he was simply a flash in the pan. But DiMaggio, back in uniform with the Yankees after serving in the Army during World War Two, liked what he saw of the big right-hander. He told the Yankees that if they ever had a chance to get Reynolds, they should take it. The Yankees followed DiMaggio's advice. That winter they traded second baseman Joe Gordon to Cleveland for Reynolds. It was one of the smartest trades the Yankees ever made.

As the 1951 baseball season opened, the Yankees were riding high. They had won two straight pennants and World Series. Reynolds had played an important part in each victory. It seemed that he did not win as many games against the second division teams as some of the other pitchers did, but when the Yankees *had* to win a game during the pennant race or the World Series, Allie usually won it for them. They used to call him "The Super Chief."

The Yankees started the season well, then fell into a slump in May, losing seven out of eight games. Reynolds won the only game during that stretch. When the Yankees began winning again, they knew that this pennant race would not be an easy one—both the Indians and the Red Sox were contending with them for first place.

On July 12 the Yankees arrived in Cleveland for an important series. The Indians had been playing well, and their great right-hander, Bob Feller, was well rested and waiting for the Yankees. Feller's fast ball was no longer as "alive" as it had been when he was younger, but he was still a marvelous pitcher. Only 12 days before the Yankees arrived, Feller had pitched the third no-hit game of his career.

Manager Stengel considered the first game of the series very important. Reynolds, of course, was his choice to pitch against Feller. Almost 40,000 Indian fans packed the ball park that night to cheer for Feller. Reynolds had his work cut out for him.

Feller was never a soft touch for any team, and on this evening he was at his best. For five innings, no Yankee batter was able to hit the ball out of the infield. The excited Cleveland fans began to wonder if their hero was on his way to another no-hitter.

But, in the excitement over Feller, the fans failed to notice that Reynolds, too, was pitching a no-hitter. The Cleveland batters were helpless against his overpowering "stuff." The first man to get a good piece of one of his pitches was right fielder Harry Simpson. In the fifth inning, Simpson timed one of Reynolds' pitches perfectly, hitting it on a line into left field, but Hank Bauer was right there to catch it.

Mickey Mantle finally shattered Feller's no-hit spell in the sixth inning. He hit a long drive to left center-field which fell safely for a double. Feller pitched his way out of trouble in that inning. But in the seventh inning, Gene Woodling, the Yankees' right fielder, hit one that neither Feller nor anyone else could do anything about. It was a high drive over the fence in right center for a home run, and the Yankees led, 1-0.

Reynolds was still in command of the Indians. In the last of the seventh, Sam Chapman, Cleveland's center fielder, hit the ball hard, but Bauer raced back to the fence in left field, leaned over and robbed him of a home run. When Reynolds returned to the Yankees' dugout after retiring the Indians in that inning, he did a very unusual thing.

One of baseball's oldest traditions requires that, when a man is pitching a no-hitter, no one on the bench will mention the fact. No matter how exciting the game or how tense the situation, everybody is supposed to pretend that nothing unusual is happening. According to the superstition, if anyone mentions the possibility of a no-hitter, the pitcher will give up a hit in the very next inning.

It is not hard to imagine the surprise of Yankee pitcher Ed Lopat when Reynolds sat down beside him at the end of the seventh inning, mopped his brow, and asked:

Reynolds was remarkably calm while pitching his no-hitter against the Indians.

"Well, Ed, what do you think? Can I pitch a no-hitter?"

Lopat was too startled to say anything at all.

In the eighth inning, every fan in the ball park knew that Reynolds was working on a no-hitter. The excitement was evident because, even though they wanted Feller to win, the Cleveland fans could not help letting out a cheer as Reynolds set down their hitters one by one. In fact, Reynolds was the calmest man in the park.

While preparing for his first pitch to one of the Indian batters, Reynolds shook off the sign from his catcher, Yogi Berra. When Yogi flashed the sign again, Reynolds called him out to the mound.

"What's the matter?" Yogi asked. "I've been signaling for the fast ball."

"I don't want to keep throwing a fast ball on the first pitch to every hitter," Reynolds said. "One of them might guess right and ruin my no-hitter."

Yogi gulped and his eyes bugged out. He had never seen a pitcher as cool as this. He returned to his position behind the plate and signaled for a curve ball.

Reynolds retired the Indians in the eighth inning. The score was still 1-0 as he came out to pitch the ninth. He struck out the first batter and got the second on an infield grounder. Now there was only one batter between him and his first no-hit game—second baseman Bobby Avila.

Reynolds was throwing hard now. He put two
fast balls past the little Mexican, but came in too
low with his next pitch. The count was one ball
and two strikes. He came back with a fast ball that
just missed the outside corner, and Avila took it
for ball two. Reynolds walked in toward the plate.

"Bobby," he asked Avila, "how do you have the
nerve to take a close pitch at a time like this?"

Avila stared at Reynolds in surprise, then grinned
and stepped back into the batters' box. He fouled
off Reynolds' next two pitches, but Allie finally put
something extra on the ball and threw it past him
for a third strike.

"What sense was there in kidding anybody?"
Reynolds later told the players and writers who had
flocked around him in the clubhouse to congratulate
him on his no-hit game. "I could see the scoreboard
lights every inning, and all those great big zeroes on
the Cleveland side never changed."

The pennant race remained close until the last
days of the season. As the Red Sox and Indians
stumbled and fell behind, the Yankees managed to
get a firm grip on first place. The final series of the
season was played on September 28, at Yankee Stadium, where the Yankees met the Red Sox in a
double-header. Stengel, anxious to clinch his fourth
straight pennant, wanted his best pitchers on the
mound, so he assigned Reynolds to pitch the first
game.

The Red Sox fielded a powerful team, which included Ted Williams and Dom DiMaggio, Joe's kid brother. Reynolds was a little wild at the start, walking DiMaggio, but Phil Rizzuto, the Yankees' alert little shortstop, executed a smart play to pull Allie out of trouble.

When Johnny Pesky hit a weak pop fly toward shortstop and DiMaggio headed back toward first base, Rizzuto let the ball drop in front of him. Then he picked it up, stepped on second base to force DiMaggio, who was trapped between the two bases, and threw to first base to put Pesky out and complete the double play.

The Yankees scored twice in their half of the first inning against the Red Sox' left-hander, Mel Parnell. They scored twice more in the third inning and went on to build up an 8-0 lead. Meanwhile, Reynolds was throwing his fast ball past the Boston hitters. He had no trouble until the seventh inning, when Ted Williams tagged one of his pitches, sending it straight at second baseman Jerry Coleman. Coleman was able to handle the ball, however, and throw Williams out.

"Ted's smack was real hard," Coleman said later. "It had plenty of 'English' on it as it skipped at me, and I overran it a little. I was lucky it was hit right at me."

With two out in that inning, Reynolds walked Clyde Vollmer, but third baseman Gil McDougald speared Billy Goodman's sharp grounder to end the inning.

The eighth inning was easy for Reynolds. As he came out to pitch the ninth inning, the crowd gave him an ovation. He needed only three more outs to enable the Yankees to clinch at least a tie for the pennant. If he succeeded, he would become the first pitcher in American League history to hurl two no-hit games in a single season.

The Red Sox sent Charley Maxwell up as a pinch hitter. He seemed determined to make Reynolds work for his no-hitter, fouling off six straight pitches. Finally Reynolds came in with a low curve ball and Maxwell hit it on the ground to Coleman at second base. Reynolds' first man was out.

Dom DiMaggio was the next batter. Allie, working too carefully, walked him. He was angry with himself, having hoped to get the first three batters out quickly, in order to prevent Ted Williams from coming to the plate. Allie got two quick strikes on Johnny Pesky, then threw a sharp curve ball that broke over the outside corner of the plate. Pesky took it for a called third strike.

With two out and a man on first base, Williams, the greatest hitter of his time, came to the plate. Reynolds would need all of his skill to retire Williams. And the Red Sox' slugger would like nothing better than to avenge his team's almost certain defeat in the pennant race by breaking up Reynolds' no-hit game.

Allie threw a half-speed pitch, which Williams took for a called strike. Now, having set up the hitter for a fast ball, Reynolds let it go with everything he had. Williams swung and hit a high pop foul behind the plate. The crowd sent up a delighted cheer as Berra tore off his mask and got set for the catch which would give Reynolds his second no-hit game. And then—Yogi dropped the ball!

The crowd groaned. Yogi beat his fist into the dirt in disgust. He had been all set to make the catch, but as the ball, twisting downward out of the gray sky, came within his reach, he misjudged it. He staggered, then sprawled out full length on the ground as the ball bounced off the edge of his big mitt. Williams would get a second, and perhaps fatal, chance to break up Reynolds' no-hitter.

Once again, the calmest person in the ball park was Reynolds. He helped Yogi back to his feet, patted him on the back and then put his arm around his shoulder.

"Okay, Yogi," he said. "We'll get him on the next pitch."

Reynolds went back to the mound, checked the base runner and fired again to the plate. Williams hit another high foul behind the plate. The big

After misjudging Ted Williams' high pop foul, Yogi Berra sees the ball bounce off his mitt.

crowd held its breath as Yogi gauged the flight of the ball. This time, it came down right into his mitt and Yogi hugged it to his chest. Reynolds had pitched his second no-hit game.

The Yankees were not to be stopped now. In the second game, they slaughtered the Red Sox, 11-3, and clinched the pennant. But clinching pennants was becoming routine business for the Yankees. When they gathered in the clubhouse afterward, they were more excited about Reynolds' no-hitter.

Reynolds' teammates congratulate him for pitching his second no-hitter.

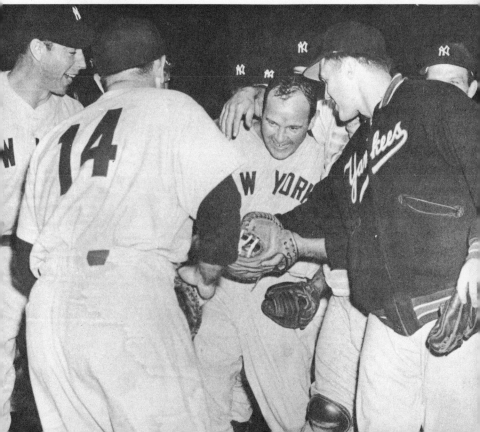

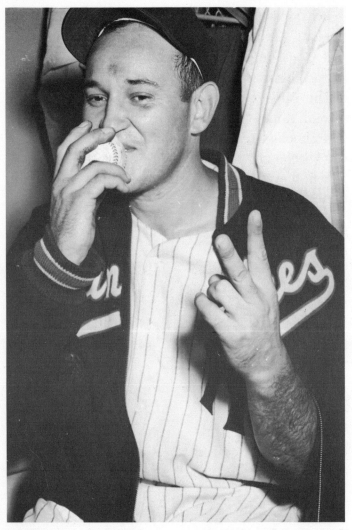

Holding up two fingers to symbolize his second no-hit game of the season, Reynolds poses for sports photographers.

"I didn't kid around today," Allie told the sports writers. "You fellows wrote your stories about what I said last time—how I kept talking about my no-hitter before I'd wrapped it up. And I got a sackful of letters from fans all over the country, bawling me out for breaking a baseball tradition."

At this point, Reynolds' face broke into a broad grin. "You'd be surprised how many people were sore about it," he said. "So this time I didn't mention it to *anybody*."

6. Bobo's Bonanza

Great pitchers do not always pitch no-hit games. Such famous pitchers as Dizzy Dean, Whitey Ford and Robin Roberts were never able to hurl no-hitters. Others—for example, Walter Johnson and Warren Spahn—did not get their first no-hitters until they had been stars for many years.

But, on the other hand, there is the curious story of a pitcher most people have probably never heard of—Alva "Bobo" Holloman.

Holloman was the most unlikely of all pitchers to get his name into the record books. In addition, he played for the most miserable of all base-

ball teams—the St. Louis Browns, who, like the
dodo bird, have been extinct for many years. Many
people would agree that Bobo Holloman belonged
with such a poor team, but they would find it hard
to believe that his name can be found in the record
books alongside such illustrious names as Koufax,
Feller and Johnson.

To understand how this happened, it is necessary
to know a little of the Browns' history. In St. Louis
they were always considered poor cousins of the
popular Cardinals. They never had enough money
to buy or sign the star players who might have
made them a winning team. Throughout their many
years in the American League, they won only one
pennant. And that happened in 1944, when the
other teams' stars were absent, fighting World War
Two. By 1953, the Browns were just about penni-
less. In fact, when the last game of the season went
into extra innings, the Browns ran out of clean base-
balls!

That year the Browns were owned by Bill Veeck.
Veeck had a sorry bunch of ballplayers, but he
was known as a "promoter." By publicity stunts
he hoped eventually to attract enough fans to the
ball park, so that he could get the money to buy
some good players. He was never able to do it, however. He ran out of money too quickly. And one
of the reasons the Browns ran out of money that
year was Bobo Holloman.

Holloman as a pitcher with the Syracuse Chiefs.

Alva Lee Holloman was born in Thomaston, Georgia, in 1926. He became a professional ball-player in 1946. He was better known as an eccentric character than as a pitcher. He had always had great confidence in himself, and he called himself "Bobo" after "Bobo" Newsom, another eccentric pitcher of the time. The only difference was that

Newsom was a good pitcher in the major leagues, and Holloman had trouble winning even in the minors.

Holloman pitched in a number of minor leagues, mostly in the South, until 1950. That year he was given a brief tryout by the Chicago Cubs, who needed pitchers very badly. Holloman wasn't quite good enough, so they sent him back to the minor leagues.

Then, in 1952, when he was 26 years old, Holloman had his best season. He won 16 games for Syracuse in the International League. That winter, in order to earn some more money, Bobo went to Puerto Rico and pitched in the winter league. He did very well, winning 20 games. He was able to brag that he had won more games that season than any other pitcher in baseball. This was probably true, because most of the successful major league pitchers in the United States did not have to seek extra work in the winter.

In St. Louis, Bill Veeck was looking around for anyone who could possibly help the Browns during the 1953 season. He had heard of Holloman and, although he wasn't sure that Bobo could make even the Browns, he was willing to take a chance on him.

So Veeck went to the Syracuse ball club and made a deal. He said that he would pay Syracuse $10,000 just for the right to keep Holloman on the Browns for a couple of months. If Holloman proved before June 15 that he really could pitch in the major leagues, then Veeck would keep him on the Browns and pay Syracuse an extra $25,000. But if Holloman was unsuccessful, Veeck would return him to Syracuse before that date, and he would not have to pay the extra $25,000.

After the Syracuse team agreed to the deal, Veeck was pleased with himself. Holloman, he thought, was worth the gamble. He couldn't be any worse than some of the pitchers already on the Browns' staff. And, even if he was, he was said to be such an eccentric fellow that the Browns might get some valuable publicity, which would be worth the $10,000 gamble.

Veeck got a shock when Holloman reported to the Browns' spring training camp. Bobo was something of a character, it was true. For one thing, whenever he walked out to the pitchers' mound to start a game, he stopped on the baseline and wrote two initials in the dirt. One was the letter "N" and the other the letter "G". They were the initials of his wife, Nan, and his son, Gary Lee. Bobo felt that scratching their initials in the dirt would somehow bring him good luck.

Veeck believed that Holloman would have a lot better luck if he got himself into shape. The Browns' owner had expected that a fellow who had been pitching for a whole year, first in Syracuse and then in Puerto Rico, would report to spring training in good physical condition. But Bobo was just plain fat. It seemed that he had spent the two or three weeks between the end of the winter league season and the opening of spring training simply sitting around and eating.

The Browns gave Bobo a fair chance. But Veeck, in his book *Veeck—as in Wreck* tells what happened:

> Bobo had charm and he had humor and he had unlimited—if sadly misplaced—confidence in himself. In spring training he was hit harder trying to get the batters out than our batting-practice pitchers who were trying to let them hit.

But Veeck, having already paid $10,000 for the use of Holloman, did not want to give up on him. He decided to keep him until June 15 and give him every possible chance. The Browns brought Bobo north when they started the season, and he became one of their relief pitchers.

Unfortunately for Bobo, once the season began, he did not do much better than he had in spring training. In four games he gave up an average of one run and two hits for every inning he pitched. Yet this did not hurt his confidence.

"I'm no relief pitcher," he kept telling Marty Marion, the Browns' manager. "Give me a chance to start a game and I'll show you something."

Marion began to look on Holloman as a sort of pest. After each game the Browns played, Bobo would come up to the manager and ask, "Am I starting tomorrow?"

Finally Veeck and Marion realized that soon they would have to make a decision about Bobo's future. Marion decided to start the big right-handed pitcher in one game, but it rained that day and the game was called off. Once again Marion told Holloman he would use him as a starting pitcher, but the same thing happened—it rained.

"Please give me a chance to start a game," Holloman said to Marion. "I promise you that you won't be sorry."

On May 6, the Browns played the Philadelphia Athletics (who were moved to Kansas City several years later). Marion decided that Holloman would be his starting pitcher.

When Bobo entered the ball park on the day of the game, he looked up at the sky. There were thick clouds overhead and he could not help worrying a little. Twice, he had been ready to pitch, and it had rained. And now it looked as if it might rain again. When he walked into the clubhouse, several of his teammates looked up.

"Well, here comes 'The Rainmaker,'" one of them said, kidding Bobo. At the moment, Bobo did not think that the remark was funny.

Then it began to rain, and the Browns' batting

practice was delayed. Bobo played a game of checkers with one of his teammates. A newspaperman looked in the clubhouse and asked Marion if they were going to play.

"We'll play tonight, no matter what," Marion said. "I've got to get this Bobo off my back."

After a little while, the rain finally stopped, and the Browns took their batting practice. Because he was going to be their starting pitcher, Holloman had his first chance to take batting practice with the regulars. He hit a couple of line drives to the wall in left field. When he left the batters' box, Bobo looked over at Marion and grinned.

"See," he said to the manager, "I told you I could hit, too."

Marion shrugged. "I've seen a lot of good hitters in practice," he said. "You've got to do it in a game to really convince me."

Finally the game began. Holloman got through the first inning without any trouble, but in the second inning Gus Zernial, the Athletics' big slugger, hit a tremendous drive to left field. Just as the ball was about to bounce off the wall, Jim Dyck, the Browns' left fielder, leaped into the air, stuck out his glove and caught it. It was one of the finest catches seen in St. Louis that season.

In the last half of the second inning, the Browns scored the first run of the game, and Holloman was the one who drove it in. Catcher Les Moss had

doubled to left. Holloman then slashed a single to
left, and Moss raced home. Bobo turned to the
Browns' coach at first base with a big grin on his
face.

"Tell the manager that was a hit," he said. He
was enjoying himself immensely.

In fact, his biggest worry at the moment was the
rain. It had started to drizzle again. The Browns
did not draw many fans even in good weather, and
the rain clouds on this evening had held the at-
tendance to less than 2,500 people. Early in the
game, Bill Veeck made an announcement over the
public address system.

"We greatly appreciate your turning out on such
a poor night," he told the crowd. "To show our
thanks, your rain checks will be good for any other
game during the coming season."

Veeck's announcement meant that, even if the
whole game was played that evening, the crowd
could hold onto their stubs and use them as free
tickets for any other game they chose. They
cheered Veeck, and went back to watching the
game.

The Browns got another run in the third inning
and led, 2-0. Every once in a while, Bobo would
begin to get tired, but then the rain would come
down and the umpires would halt the game for a
few minutes. This always gave Bobo a chance to
get his breath before going back to pitching.

By the fifth inning, he still had not given up a hit. But in the fifth, the Athletics came close. Allie Clark hit a long drive that no St. Louis player could have caught, but at the last moment the ball curved foul before going over the fence. A moment later, Zernial hit a ground ball back to Holloman. Bobo bent down for it, and it rolled into his glove and then rolled right out again. The crowd, already aware that Bobo had not yet given up a hit, sent up a chant:

"Error! Error! Error!"

And that was how the official scorer called it. Bobo still had not given up a hit.

After the Browns scored again in their half of the fifth, Bobo had another hair-raising moment in the sixth inning. Joe Astroth, the Athletics' catcher, bunted just along the third base line. Neither Holloman nor the Browns' third baseman, Bob Elliott, had a chance to field the ball before Astroth reached first base.

"Let it go! Let it go!" Marion shouted from the Browns' dugout.

The ball rolled slowly up the third base line. Bobo trotted along beside it, waving everybody away so that no one would touch it. He pleaded with it to roll foul. And slowly it curved into foul territory, where Bobo scooped it up in his glove before it had a chance to roll fair again. It was simply a foul strike, and Astroth had to come back to the plate and bat again. This time Bobo got him out easily, and the fans breathed a sigh of relief.

In the last of the seventh inning, when Holloman came to bat with two runners on base, the small crowd gave him a tremendous round of applause. Bobo kept the cheers coming by driving in both runners with a solid single to left. The Browns now led by a score of 6-0, and Holloman had driven in three of the runs.

But he was struggling now. Luckily, several hard line drives off the bats of Philadelphia hitters were caught by St. Louis fielders. Often Bobo went to counts of 3-2 on the batters, but he always managed to get the important pitch over the plate. In the eighth inning, shortstop Billy Hunter made a great play behind second base and took a sure base hit away from the Athletics' Joe Astroth.

"When Hunter made that great play, I knew right then that I was going to pitch a no-hitter," Holloman said later. "I was still nervous, sure—but I knew I was going to pitch a no-hitter."

By the ninth inning, Bobo was throwing mostly sinker balls, his most effective pitch. Before each pitch, the crowd would become deathly silent. Even the boys selling peanuts and soft drinks stopped to watch what was going to happen. And Bobo gave everybody in the ball park nervous fits.

With only three outs to collect for his no-hitter, Bobo began the ninth inning by walking a pinch hitter, Elmer Valo. With Eddie Joost at bat, Holloman still couldn't get his sinker ball over the plate and he walked him, too. The Athletics had two runners on base and nobody out. At that moment, Harry Brecheen, the Browns' pitching coach, who had once been a fine pitcher himself, walked out to the mound.

"Are you getting tired, Bobo?" Brecheen asked.

"No, I'm okay," Holloman said.

"Well, slow down," Brecheen told him. "You're pitching too fast. And you're not following through properly with your pitches. Now take it easy."

Holloman, whose uniform was soaked with perspiration, nodded and got ready to face the next batter. He was Dave Philley, who had a .354 batting average for the Athletics. But Bobo got his sinker where he wanted it, and Philley hit the ball on the ground to Bobby Young, the second baseman, who started a double play.

With only one out to go, Bobo found himself still in trouble. He walked Loren Babe, and now there were runners on first and third. Eddie Robinson, the Athletics' most powerful hitter, was at the plate. Holloman made his first pitch a little too good, and Robinson hit a tremendous smash over the fence—but foul!

Les Moss, the catcher, came out to the mound to talk to Bobo.

"That pitch was a curve ball," Moss said. "He'll

probably expect us to throw him a fast ball this time so let's cross him up and give him another curve."

Bobo nodded. He got his curve ball over, and Robinson hit an easy fly to Vic Wertz in right field. The crowd sent up a victorious cheer even before the Browns' right fielder caught the ball.

Not until Holloman got to the clubhouse did he realize how great his achievement was. He knew he had pitched a no-hitter, of course. But then he found out that he was the first man in modern baseball history to pitch a no-hit game in his first major league start.

"I was just praying and hoping," was the way Bobo explained his no-hitter.

His wife, Nan, and little Gary Lee were there to greet him at the clubhouse door. Tears were running down his wife's cheeks.

"Wonderful . . . wonderful," was the only word she could say.

Bobo grinned down at Gary Lee and gave his son the ball that Vic Wertz had caught for the final out of the game.

It would be nice to report that Bobo Holloman went on from there to become a star. But the truth is that his no-hitter against the Athletics was his only bright moment in the majors. In his next start, he lasted less than two innings. He never again pitched a complete game for the Browns.

Bobo is surrounded by Brownie players as he leaves the field after pitching a no-hitter in his first major league start.

However, since Bobo had pitched a no-hit game, Bill Veeck could not very well send him back to the minor leagues before the June 15 deadline. He had to keep him on the team, and that meant he had to pay Syracuse an extra $25,000.

By July, Bobo was pitching so poorly that Veeck was forced to sell him to another minor league team, and he received only $7,500 for him. It had cost Veeck a total of $35,000 to obtain Bobo from Syracuse. After subtracting the $7,500, one sees that, in effect, the Browns had paid $27,500 for a no-hitter. It was something that the bankrupt team could not afford. A year later, they left St. Louis forever and became the Baltimore Orioles.

A total of $27,500 for a no-hit game sounds like a great deal of money, but any other ball club in baseball would have considered it a bargain.

7. Cheers for a Villain

Worries piled up for the Dodgers early in 1956. The year before, they had won the pennant and the World Series. They had started 1956 confidently, but soon they realized that they could expect plenty of trouble. Some of their stars were getting old. They needed at least one more good pitcher. In addition, they didn't seem to be as good as they had been the year before, while their most likely rivals, the Milwaukee Braves and the Cincinnati Reds, were much stronger.

One day, just before the middle of May, the telephone rang in the office of E. J. "Buzzie" Bavasi, the vice-president of the Dodgers. The caller was

Hank Greenberg, who ran the Cleveland Indians. He wanted to discuss the second of two exhibition games the Dodgers and Indians were playing during the season. They had played the first one in Jersey City, New Jersey, only a few days before.

When the two baseball executives got through talking about the exhibition games, the conversation turned to pitching. The Dodgers needed pitchers, and that was the one department in which the Indians had more men than they needed.

"Look, Buzzie," Greenberg said, "I've got to get rid of one of my older pitchers so some of the younger fellows will have a chance. I've got two old pitchers on the team now—Bob Feller and Sal Maglie. Feller has been a hero here in Cleveland for a long time, and we're never going to sell him. That means I've got to get rid of Maglie. He can still pitch a little bit. He might be able to help you."

Bavasi was interested. He knew that Maglie wasn't pitching much in Cleveland, but he had pitched against the Dodgers in the first exhibition game and had done very well.

"Let me call you back," Bavasi said to Greenberg.

Then he called the Dodgers' manager, Walter Alston.

"We've got a chance to buy Sal Maglie," he told Alston. "What do you think?"

"He looked mighty good to me in Jersey City,"

Alston said. "I'd say grab him."

Then Bavasi called the Dodgers' shortstop, Pee Wee Reese, at his home in Brooklyn.

"Pee Wee, you hit against Maglie in that exhibition game, and you also used to hit against him when he pitched for the Giants," Bavasi said. "What did you think of him the other night?"

"Why?" Reese asked.

"We have a chance to get him."

"Buzzie, I honestly couldn't see any difference between Maglie when he was great and Maglie the other night," Reese said. "He looked like the same guy to me."

"Do you think we should gamble on him?"

"I'd like to see Maglie on our side," Reese said.

Bavasi called Greenberg back and made the deal. It was one of the most astonishing deals in baseball history. When the news was announced in the papers, most people thought it was a publicity stunt. An old pitcher like Maglie couldn't possibly help the Dodgers!

Those people who thought it was a publicity stunt had good reason, for it seemed unbelievable that Maglie would ever wear a Dodgers' uniform. For years Sal Maglie had been the most hated man in Brooklyn. The mention of his name was enough to make any good Dodger fan tear his hair out.

The reason for this was simple. When the Dodgers and the Giants used to play in Brooklyn and

New York, both teams were fierce rivals, just as they are today in their new homes at Los Angeles and San Francisco. The Dodgers had always had powerful hitters, but somehow, whenever Maglie appeared on the pitcher's mound for the Giants, Brooklyn was helpless.

To the Dodgers, Maglie was a sinister-looking fellow. He always seemed to need a shave, and his dark, hooded eyes made him look as if he were staring down at the batter and thinking about cutting his throat—which was just what he did, figuratively. If the batter got too close to the plate, Maglie would throw a fast ball just under his chin and drive him back. Then he would come back with his amazing curve ball over the outside corner, and the batter, standing away from the plate, would not be able to get any power into his swing.

"His curve ball is just *different* from anybody else's," Roy Campanella, the Dodgers' slugging catcher, once said. "It's positively the best I ever hit at."

Thus Maglie, during the years he was with the Giants, made life miserable for both the Dodgers and their fans. The Dodgers could usually take apart any other pitcher in the league. But not Maglie. The Dodgers estimated that he had cost them at least two pennants. They were infuriated because he not only beat them, but he looked so *mean* while he went about it. Whenever he appeared at Ebbets

Maglie is shown on the mound for the New York Giants.

Field, the crowd booed Maglie unmercifully. And then they sat back and watched him tie their heroes into knots.

Then, in 1955, Maglie injured his back. It seemed that his career was over. Whenever he tried to pitch, he was knocked out of the box. Even the Dodgers beat him!

So the Giants sold him to the Cleveland Indians. But the Indians had so many good pitchers that they seldom used him. Everybody believed that Maglie was through as a major league pitcher. That was why it was hard to believe that he would come back to Brooklyn in a Dodger uniform.

Manager Alston planned to use Sal as a "spot" pitcher. This meant that he would not make him one of his regular starting pitchers, but would let him start a game once in a while when the team had several double-headers scheduled in a week or when one of the regular pitchers was hurt.

Sal pitched several times for the Dodgers. He did not do very well, but the Dodgers were so short of pitchers that they would use anybody who could get the ball over the plate. And Maglie's control was usually good.

The Dodgers were playing poorly. They went to Chicago, and the Cubs, who were in last place, beat them three straight times. Then the Dodgers went to Milwaukee to play a series with the Braves, who looked as if they might win the pennant.

Alston didn't know which of his pitchers to start against the Braves.

On the morning of the first game, Maglie came to him. "I know you're planning to use me later in the week," Sal said. "But would I do you more good tonight?"

"Heck, yes," Alston said.

Maglie shut out the Braves, 3-0, and pulled the Dodgers out of their slump. From then on Sal worked more often, but he didn't get credit for winning many games. After pitching five or six good innings, he was usually taken out for a pinch hitter, since it seemed that the Dodgers never scored many runs when he was on the mound. He started eight games in six weeks, losing three times. However, during those three games, he didn't get much support from his team, who scored a total of only four runs.

Both the Brooklyn players and their fans were beginning to think differently about him by this time. Once they got to know Maglie, they learned he was not such a bad fellow after all. He was, it is true, what they call in baseball a "loner." He was one of the few Dodger players who did not live in Brooklyn during the season. He had pitched for the Giants for so many years that he preferred to live across the bridge in Manhattan. After every home game, Sal would take his shower, put on his clothes, collect his watch, wallet and other valuables from the clubhouse man and leave the ball park alone.

But while he was at the park, he was a big help to the team. Because he was able to pitch once in a while, he took the load off the regular pitchers. He also gave tips on pitching to the younger men on the staff. As a rule, however, he kept his distance from the other players. But gradually, even though they used to dislike him when he pitched for the Giants, the Dodgers were beginning to admire him.

"Maglie molded our pitching staff, and then he educated it," Jackie Robinson, the Dodgers' second baseman, said.

"Is he a nice guy?" somebody asked Robinson.

"I don't know about that," Jackie said, "but he's sure a good pitcher."

Roy Campanella, who used to have fits trying to hit Maglie's curve ball, grinned when Sal's name was mentioned. "Let me tell you, buddy," he said, "that curve ball's a lot easier to catch than it is to hit."

"It's a pleasure to play shortstop behind Maglie," Pee Wee Reese said. "He's got this game down to such a science you pretty nearly always know just where the ball's going to be hit when he's pitching."

Towards the end of July, the Dodgers' bid for the pennant was being bitterly contested by both the Reds and the Braves. It did not look as if the Dodg-

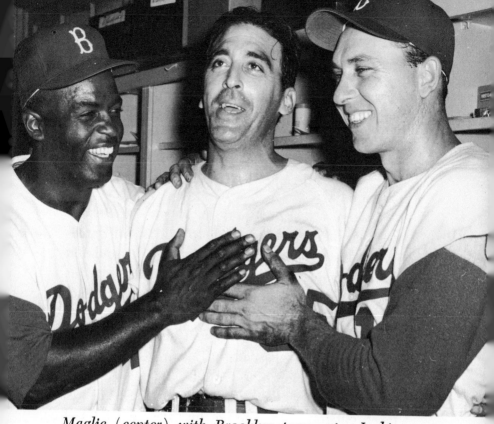

Maglie (center) with Brooklyn teammates Jackie Robinson and Gil Hodges.

ers could hold them off much longer. All of a sudden, Maglie was asked to pitch every fourth day. This was something that no one believed possible for a 39-year-old pitcher who had a history of back trouble.

"From the time the Giants sold me in July of 1955 until I began pitching regularly for the Dodgers a year later, I was pretty much on vacation," Maglie explained. "Did it help me? Let's say this— it sure didn't *hurt* me. I came back stronger than

I'd been in years. The rest strengthened my arm
and my back. But I've found that when my arm gets
strong it gets tight, too, and then I don't have good
control. Only regular work sharpens my control,
and regular work means pitching with only three
or four days' rest."

The most amazing part of Maglie's comeback
was that he not only was able to win the *big* games
for the Dodgers, but he was able to go out and win
the *little* games in between as well. Sal began his
heavy schedule on July 28, beating the Cubs, 6-3.

From then until the end of the season, he started
15 games for the Dodgers, won ten and lost only
two, and had an earned-run average of 1.88. He
lost the two games by scores of 3-2 and 2-1. In the
three games in which he did not win or lose but was
taken out for a pinch hitter, he gave up a total of
only two earned runs.

On September 11, against the Braves, Sal pitched
one of his most important games of the year. It was
the start of a two-game series, the last of the year
between these two pennant contenders. The Braves
arrived at Ebbets Field, one game ahead of the
Dodgers.

For seven innings, Maglie kept the Braves under
control, and the Dodgers were leading, 2-1. Eddie
Mathews had given the Braves their only run, with
a homer in the second inning. The Dodgers had
gotten their two runs in the fourth inning, when

the aging Maglie came to the plate with the bases filled and singled sharply to left.

Then, in the eighth inning, with two out, the Braves put the tying run on third base. Maglie looked tired, and the next batter was the Braves' slugger, Ed Mathews. Manager Alston came out of the dugout to talk to Sal.

"What do you want to do?" Alston asked him. "I've got a couple of relief pitchers all ready if you're tired."

"I got to pitch to this guy," Maglie said.

Alston turned around and went back to the dugout. Maglie pitched to Mathews and got him out. The Dodgers went on to win the game.

But the other pitchers on the staff were having trouble winning games. And the Braves stayed even with the Dodgers. As the season went into its final week, the Dodgers had their backs to the wall. Every game was important now.

On September 25, the Phillies arrived at Ebbets Field for a series, and Alston chose Maglie to pitch the first game. For once, Maglie received solid batting support. The Dodgers scored three times in the second inning, two of the runs coming across when Campanella hit a long home run into the left field stands. In the third inning they added two more runs as the result of a wild throw and built up a 5-0 lead.

That was the score as the Phillies came to bat in

After pitching a no-hitter against the Phillies, Maglie (35) is escorted to the dugout by a special police guard.

the ninth inning. For the 15,000 fans in the stands at Ebbets Field, the drama of the pennant race was now secondary to the personal drama of this aging right-hander who seemed on the verge of pitching the first no-hit game of his career. Only two Philadelphia batters had reached base, both of them on walks.

"I thought I had a good chance to pitch the no-hitter when I walked out there in the ninth," Maglie said. "The bottom part of the Phillies' batting order was coming up. I had good stuff on the ball. The fans were all yelling but I said to myself, just ignore it—just concentrate on the hitters."

The first batter was Frankie Baumholtz. Maglie pitched to him and he hit a high pop foul over near the Dodgers' dugout.

Maglie saw that the wind was blowing the ball toward the stands and thought that Campanella wouldn't be able to get it. But Campy never gave up. He kept right on chasing the ball to the edge of the dugout, reached out and, tumbling down the dugout steps, managed to hold onto the ball for a sensational catch.

The next batter was Harvey Haddix, a pitcher who was also a good hitter. Maglie got two quick strikes on him.

"Haddix was standing away from the plate," Maglie said later. "I wanted that third strike. I wanted to hit the outside corner. I thought if I could get it there, there wouldn't be any way for Haddix to get around on the ball."

Maglie got the pitch just where he wanted to, and Haddix struck out. The next batter was Richie Ashburn. Maglie got two quick strikes on him, too. On his next pitch, he tried to make his curve break low and inside, but the ball got away from him. It hit Ashburn on the foot, and Richie went to first base.

Marv Blaylock now stood between Sal and his no-hitter. Maglie threw him a fast ball over the outside corner and Blaylock hit a grounder to Jim Gilliam.

"I watched the ball bounce all the way," Maglie said. "I watched every darn hop until Gilliam got it and Hodges grabbed his throw and the umpire's arm went up for the out."

Maglie had his no-hitter. He also had given the Dodgers the spark they needed to keep them going through that last rugged week of the season. By week's end, the Dodgers were once more the champions of the National League.

8. The Nightrider Makes History

Strangely enough, within two weeks after Sal Maglie had pitched his own no-hit game, he and the Dodgers met their downfall at the hands of another no-hit pitcher—Don Larsen.

It would be hard to imagine two pitchers who were more different than Maglie and Larsen. Maglie, a slender veteran, had never possessed an overwhelming fast ball. He had learned the art of pitching after many years of experience, hard work and listening to others. Larsen, a big, broad-shouldered young man, had a good fast ball to begin with. Yet he never made the most of his talent. Though he stayed in the major leagues for some years, he could be compared more closely to Bobo Holloman, because he enjoyed only one moment of glory.

Perhaps Larsen was born with too much talent. His success as a schoolboy may have convinced him that he could go through life in his own happy-go-lucky way, and the triumphs would come rolling in just as they had on the sandlots of San Diego, California.

Donald James Larsen was born in Michigan City, Indiana, in 1929, but his family moved to San Diego when he was still a small boy.

"Don was kind of a wild kid, and he got in a couple of minor scrapes, but he was always likeable," an old friend of his has said. "I remember he used to have a paper route. He was crazy about cats and dogs, and sometimes when he came home from delivering his papers he'd be dragging along some stray animal he had found. His mother wouldn't let him keep it and it would make him unhappy."

Don learned to throw a baseball in the basement of his home, with his father serving as catcher. But he was always a big, rangy kid, and he first became known around San Diego as a basketball player. He was a good shooter, and he was large enough to be able to grab rebounds off the boards.

But one day a scout for the St. Louis Browns saw Don play baseball. Larsen could throw hard, run fast and hit the ball farther than anybody else in

Larsen as a pitcher with the Browns.

town. The scout didn't know whether Don should be a pitcher or an outfielder, but he knew that he should be a ballplayer.

Don signed a contract with the Browns, whose greatest need was for pitchers, and so he became a pitcher. He didn't do very well in the minor leagues, though. It looked as if he was going to be a failure, and it must have been with a sigh of relief that he entered the Army in 1951.

But, in the Army, Larsen was a star once more. Playing with a service team in Hawaii, he pitched so well and hit so many home runs that the fans said he was the best ballplayer they had seen in Hawaii since the great major leaguers had come to the Pacific during World War Two.

When he got out of the Army in 1953, Don was told by the Browns to report to their spring training camp. Among the other rookies in camp was pitcher Bobo Holloman, who had reported fat and out of shape. Larsen, coming out of the Army, was in much better condition, and he made a good impression on the Browns. Satchel Paige, the seemingly ageless pitcher who was also with the Browns that year, was especially pleased.

"That kid oughta be the greatest!" he told a reporter after watching Larsen pitch in an exhibition game.

When the season began, however, Satchel turned out to be a better pitcher than a prophet, because

Larsen didn't seem to be a big league pitcher at all.

Although Larsen was getting bombed on the mound, he was having much better luck when he got a bat in his hands. During the 1953 season, he set an all-time major league record for a pitcher by making seven straight hits. But by August 15 he had won only two games and had lost eleven. Then, toward the end of the season, he began to pitch well, winning five of his last six games.

The next season, the Browns were moved out of St. Louis and they became the Baltimore Orioles. The change of scene didn't help Larsen. In fact, he had one of the worst seasons any major league pitcher has ever had. He won only three games and lost 21. His manager, Jimmy Dykes, wasn't very happy with either Don's record or his conduct. Unfortunately, Don liked to read comic books and stay up late at night. He started to call himself "The Nightrider," a nickname that celebrated both his late hours and his favorite comic-book adventures.

"The only thing Larsen fears is sleep," Manager Dykes said.

In 1955 the Orioles finally got rid of Larsen, but they really did him a favor by trading him to the Yankees. In those days, the Yankees won the pennant almost every year. However, Larsen clung to his old habits, and some of his new teammates started calling him "Gooneybird." Casey Stengel, who managed the Yankees then, had always liked big strong pitchers who could throw fast balls. But he refused to put up with any nonsense from a player who wasn't pitching very well. He decided to send Larsen back to the minor leagues.

Don was disgusted. He thought about quitting baseball and going home. Then Mickey Mantle took him aside and talked to him.

"They sent me back to the minor leagues a few years ago," Mantle told Larsen, "but when I started to play well again they brought me back. You'll be back up here with the Yankees in a couple of weeks."

Mickey was right. Larsen pitched well in the minors, and the Yankees brought him back to finish the season with them. He even pitched in the World Series that year, but he was knocked out of the box by the Dodgers. His only memorable deed occurred when he had a bat in his hands. He hit a high pop foul which drifted into the box seats near the Yankees' dugout and bounced off the head of the Yankees' owner, Del Webb.

In 1956 Larsen had a fairly good season, winning 11 games and losing five. But in his last game of the season, he made a sudden change in the way he delivered the ball to the plate—he stopped using a windup!

The Yankees were playing the Red Sox in Boston. Larsen suspected that the Red Sox were getting a good look at how he held the ball for each pitch, which would enable them to tell whether he was going to throw a fast ball or a curve ball. In order to give them less time to see how he was holding the ball, Don decided to pitch without going into a windup. He simply hauled off and threw the ball.

He was very pleased with the results, because he shut out the Red Sox that day. He decided to pitch the same way in the coming World Series. When one of Don's teammates asked him what had given him the idea of pitching without a windup, Larsen grinned and said, "The ghouls gave me the message." He was referring, of course, to the revolting creatures he had discovered in his comic-book reading.

The ghouls weren't much help when Don made his first start against the Dodgers. He had gone to bed early to get a good night's sleep before pitching, but he was knocked out of the box in the second inning and the Dodgers won, 13-8. Afterward, Larsen told somebody how unhappy he was about the game.

"That's the last time *I'll* ever go to bed early," he said.

The World Series was tied at two games for each team when manager Stengel gave Don another chance to pitch. Everybody believed that the team which won on October 8 would also win the Series.

The Dodgers were using their ace pitcher, Sal Maglie, who had beaten the Yankees in the first game.

The night before the game, Don kept his promise to himself. He did not go to bed early, but went out with an old friend. During the evening, the talk got around to the sports car which *Sport* Magazine was going to give to the outstanding player in the World Series.

"Wouldn't it be great to win that car!" Don said to his friend. "Who knows? Maybe I'll beat Maglie tomorrow and hit a grand slam home run."

Then, feeling more confident already, he said, "Why, I'm just liable to go out there and pitch a no-hitter!"

Since no one had ever pitched a no-hitter in a World Series game, his friend did not take Don very seriously.

The next day, nearly 65,000 people jammed Yankee Stadium for this important game. Both Maglie and Larsen (who was still pitching without a wind-up) got off to good starts, though a couple of the Dodgers hit savage line drives in the early innings. One close call came in the second inning, when Jackie Robinson slashed a ball toward left field. But third baseman Andy Carey, leaping high in the air, deflected it toward shortstop, where Gil McDougald pounced on it and threw Robinson out.

But no runner on either side reached base until the last half of the fourth inning when Mickey

Mantle connects with Maglie's fifth pitch to send the ball into the right-field stands.

Mantle came to bat for the Yankees. Maglie tried
to set Mantle up for an inside fast ball by throwing
him four straight pitches on the outside. Two of
them were a little wide for called balls, and Mickey
fouled off the other two for strikes. Now, with the
count two balls and two strikes, Maglie figured that
Mantle would be looking for another wide pitch.
He threw a fast ball over the inside corner, but
Mantle was ready and hit it into the right field
stands for a home run. The Yankees led, 1-0.

At that point, Maglie's great arm seemed at last
to have run down. Almost everything he served up
for the next two innings was turned into a line drive,
and only the Dodgers' alert defense kept the Yankees from scoring more than one additional run.
After that, Larsen coasted along with his 2-0 lead,
getting the Dodgers' hitters out with seemingly
ridiculous ease.

But Maglie was as heroic in defeat as he had been
all year in victory. He pulled himself together and
stopped the Yankees cold. It was still a close ball
game. More than that, the fans suddenly realized
that Larsen had not permitted a Dodger batter to
reach base in any way whatever.

Over the years, although there had never been a
no-hitter in the World Series, there had been a
number pitched in the regular season. But since
1922 no one had pitched a *perfect* game in any big
league game. A perfect game is one in which a

pitcher does not give up a hit, and also does not let a batter reach base by means of a walk, a hit batsman, an error or by any other means.

Some time during the seventh inning, Larsen became aware of what was going on. "By then the guys on the bench wouldn't even look at me when I came back between innings," he said later.

In the stands, all but the most avid Dodger fans were rooting for Larsen to pitch a perfect game. Don's roommate, Rip Coleman, who couldn't stand the tension any longer, left the Yankees' dugout and began to pace up and down under the stands. A groundskeeper came along and smiled brightly at Coleman.

"Larsen's pitching a no-hitter," he told Coleman, as if he didn't already know it.

Coleman just glared at him.

Over in the Brooklyn dugout, Maglie watched his rival's progress. "I know just how he felt," Maglie said after the game. "I know it sounds silly, but I wanted us to beat him somehow without spoiling his performance."

On the Yankees' bench, the players fidgeted nervously. "I never had so many assistant managers," Stengel said. "On every pitch the guys were hollering out to the fielders, telling them where to play the Dodger hitters."

Probably the most nervous men in the stadium were the three official scorers. They hoped that no batter would hit a tricky hopper and reach base, causing a situation that might require them to make a difficult decision about whether the play should be scored as a hit or an error. And in the radio and television booths, the announcers were trying to tell the fans exactly what was going on without mentioning the words "no-hitter" or "perfect game." If they broke the old baseball superstition and somebody did get a hit off Larsen, they would certainly be accused by many listeners of having "jinxed" him.

Larsen's mother, who should have been more interested in his progress than anyone else, did not even turn on her television set. Her friends kept her notified about the game while she prayed alone in her apartment.

"I never watch him on television when he pitches," she told a reporter. "Seems like every time I do, he loses."

When Larsen came to bat in the last half of the eighth inning, the big crowd came to its feet and gave him an ovation. Maglie struck out Larsen and, finishing up in his own minor blaze of glory, also struck out the other two Yankee batters he faced that inning. Then Larsen took a deep breath, hitched up his pants and walked out to the mound to defend his 2-0 lead and his no-hitter.

"The Dodgers are still in the game," Larsen's catcher, Yogi Berra, said to him. "Get the first guy out. That's the main thing."

The first man was a dangerous batter, Carl Furillo. Several years before, in the ninth inning of a World Series game at Yankee Stadium, the right-handed Furillo had poked a pitch to the opposite field for a home run and had tied up a tight game. He seemed to be trying to do the same thing now. He fouled off four different pitches into the stands behind first base. Finally, Larsen put another fast ball over the plate, and Furillo hit a high fly to the right fielder, who caught it easily.

The next batter was Roy Campanella, who was always a threat to hit a home run. Campy belted Larsen's first pitch toward the upper stands in left field. But, as the crowd gasped, the ball sailed into foul territory. Then Larsen threw his only curve ball that inning, and Campanella grounded out to the second baseman. Two out.

Now the Dodgers sent up a pinch hitter, Dale Mitchell. Larsen knew all about Mitchell, because he had pitched against him many times when Mitchell was with the Cleveland Indians. Dale was not a home-run hitter. Still, he was a dangerous man in this situation because he liked to punch hits through the infield.

"Mitchell really scared me," Larsen said after the game. "Looking back on it though, I know how much pressure he must have been under. He must have been paralyzed. That made two of us."

In the ninth inning Larsen delivers the third strike to Dodger pinch-hitter Dale Mitchell for the final out. The scoreboard registers a string of zeros for Brooklyn.

The crowd sent up a groan as Larsen's first pitch went wide. Don came back with a slider and umpire Babe Pinelli called it a strike. Then, firing hard, Larsen got his fast ball over the plate. Mitchell swung at it and missed for strike two.

Larsen was trying to overpower the batter now. He fired another fast ball, but Mitchell got a piece of it and fouled it back into the stands. By now the crowd was screaming with every pitch. Don looked toward the plate and caught Berra's signal for still another fast ball. He mumbled a brief prayer to himself: "Please get me through this." Then he pitched.

It was over the outside corner. Mitchell stood there, just as Larsen described him after the game —paralyzed. He watched the ball go by and, when the umpire threw up his arm to signal "Strike Three!" a tremendous burst of noise came from the stands. Don Larsen had become the first man in baseball history to pitch a no-hit game in the World Series.

After the game, newspapermen from all over the country crowded into the Yankees' clubhouse to interview the new hero. They took his picture and asked him all sorts of questions. Some of them were intelligent questions. One, at least, was pretty silly.

"Don," one of the reporters asked, "was this the best game you ever pitched?"

Don didn't even have to answer, because it may

have been the best game that *any* player has ever pitched. Larsen never again showed such form. But on that one October day, he put his name into the record books in a place where not even Walter Johnson, Bob Feller and Sandy Koufax are mentioned. A World Series is baseball's greatest event, and Don Larsen pitched its greatest game.

Yogi Berra jumps into Larsen's arms after helping him to pitch the first no-hitter in World Series history.

9. A Boy's Best Friend

Big league ball players are just like most other human beings. They like to take full credit for their success, often forgetting the help they received from other people while they were on the way up. But Bill Monbouquette never forgot.

"Gus Hennessy is the best friend I've ever had," Monbouquette has said. "Probably the best friend I'll *ever* have."

There are a lot of Gus Hennessy's in this country. They are men who work at all sorts of jobs, but in their spare time they serve as Little League coaches or managers of sandlot teams, helping to make better ballplayers out of the boys they work

with. Gus Hennessy came along at just the right
time in Bill Monbouquette's life.

Bill was born in Medford, Massachusetts, in 1936.
His father was of French-Canadian descent and his
last name (pronounced Mon-boo-KET) means, in
French, "my little flowers." But there was nothing
flowery about Bill when he was growing up in
Medford.

"I liked to think I was a tough kid," Monbouquette once said. "Not bad, but wild, and I hung
around with a wild crowd. We broke windows and
that sort of stuff. I wouldn't take anything from anybody."

Monbouquette, or "Monbo," as the newspapermen began to call him when he reached the major
leagues, met Hennessy at St. Raphael's Church in
Medford.

"I got to know Gus real well and he straightened
me out," Bill said. "He convinced me that I had a
future in baseball. He told me I was wasting a lot
of time and that I'd better stop hanging around
street corners with guys who were only going to
get me into trouble."

In many ways, Monbouquette and Hennessy were
very much alike, so they had a certain respect for
each other right from the start.

"I could look up to Gus," Bill said. "He was a
fellow who never had it easy. He was an orphan

kid. Grew up in an institution, and never had much athletic ability of his own. Nobody ever gave him any breaks. But in his own way he had a lot of toughness, and he'd always stand up for you."

Hennessy had much the same thing to say about Monbouquette.

"I guess Bill was about thirteen years old when I first saw him. I'd just gotten out of the service and I began working with the kids at St. Raphael's. Monbouquette was a third baseman then. He hadn't filled out when I first saw him, but I liked the way he played and the way he carried himself. Just as he said, he wouldn't take anything from anybody."

Hennessy earned his living as a milkman. He spent most of his spare time at the sandlot ball fields around Medford. When Monbouquette took up pitching, Gus was helping to run the Junior American Legion's baseball program. He thought that Bill showed a lot of promise, and soon he had him pitching Junior Legion ball.

"I guess I played more ball than most kids around there," Bill once told a reporter. "When I was fourteen, the manager of a semipro team asked me if I wanted to pitch for his club. It was a fast league—good high school players, and even a few guys who'd played some pro ball but hadn't made the grade."

Bill quickly learned what it was like to be thrown in over his head. One afternoon the manager started him in a game against an Army team from Fort Devens, Massachusetts.

"I think the final score was 24-2," Bill said. "The manager let me go all the way. People in the stands were hollering, 'Take the kid out! You'll ruin him!' But I was only fourteen and I could pitch all day. Later the manager said it was good for me.

"'I kept you in so you could strengthen your arm,' he told me. 'A beating won't hurt you.'

"'Beating?' I said. 'Heck, it was *murder*.'"

About this time, a major league scout saw Bill pitch in Medford. Monbouquette, of course, was still much too young to sign a contract, but the scout liked what he saw of him. He told Bill, however, that he would do better if he switched from throwing the ball with a sidearm motion to throwing it directly overhand. Gus Hennessy helped the youngster to make the change. They both believe the change in his pitching motion had a lot to do with Bill's eventual success.

By the time he was a junior in high school, Bill had grown into a husky boy. People in the Boston area were beginning to talk about this fellow from Medford with the strong right arm and the fierce will to win. Tryouts were being held in Boston at that time for the Hearst All-Stars, sponsored by the Hearst chain of newspapers. Every year this team was selected from among the best high school

While a junior in high school, Monbouquette won the Lou Gehrig Trophy as the most outstanding player in the 1954 Hearst All-Star Game.

players in the country to play a charity game in New York City.

Bill went to the tryouts and became one of the finalists from the Boston area. Then, to his surprise, he was cut from the squad.

"I was hopping mad, and so was Gus," Monbouquette said. " 'You can't cut this kid,' Gus told the Hearst people. 'He's the best pitcher you've got.' So later they said O.K., they'd give me another chance, but I thought they were only trying to calm us down. Then I got a telegram to come to Fenway Park in Boston and pitch in the tryout game that would decide which players would go to New York from our area."

Monbouquette made the coaches' decision an easy one. He faced six batters in the tryout game, and struck out all of them! In a warm-up game at Gloucester, before going to New York, he struck out 12 batters in four innings.

After arriving in New York to join the United States All-Stars, Bill was so impressive in practice that he was named the starting pitcher for the big game. He pitched two innings, fanned five of the six batters he faced and was awarded the Lou Gehrig Trophy as the game's outstanding player. Mrs. Gehrig, the great first baseman's widow, presented the trophy to Bill during ceremonies after the game.

Now the big league scouts were flocking around

the young pitcher. Because Bill's father, who was an
electrician, didn't know much about baseball he decided to let Gus Hennessy handle the arrangements
for his son's professional contract.

"My folks didn't know anything about the business end of baseball," Bill said. "In fact, they were
wonderful through the whole thing. They'd never
tell me when they were coming to see me play,
and this kept me from being nervous. They never
put themselves forward like a lot of parents do.
Sometimes my father would just say, 'Nice game,
son,' when I'd come home after pitching, and that
was the first time I'd realize that they'd been at the
ball park."

So Gus Hennessy talked to all the big league
scouts who were interested in Monbouquette. The
Detroit Tigers and the Chicago Cubs especially
wanted to sign Bill, but in the end he and Gus decided to accept the Red Sox' offer. After all, the
Red Sox had always been the "home team" for Bill,
and he was proud to join them.

"The Red Sox wanted Bill to stay around Boston
and pitch batting practice for them all summer,"
Hennessy said. " 'Uh-uh!' I told them. 'This kid
has to get his feet wet pitching in pro ball. He's got
to get experience.' "

As soon as Bill had been graduated from high
school, the Red Sox sent him to one of their minor
league teams. In his first start, he was beaten nearly

as badly as he had been by the Fort Devens team.

"I got bombed but I wasn't discouraged," Bill said. "I knew that Gus had been right, and that the only way I was going to learn was to pitch against all kinds of opposition, and take the good with the bad."

Bill had his troubles for a couple of seasons. Often he felt he was not being used as much as he should be, and that he was being passed over for less-talented pitchers. Whenever he began to feel that way, no matter where he was, Bill always went right to a telephone.

"He'd call me when he got down in the dumps," Hennessy said, "and the next day I'd go over to the Red Sox office in Boston and find out what the story was. The Red Sox' minor league department was always very nice about it. They'd explain things to me and tell me that Monbo still figured in their plans for the future. Then I'd call Monbo back and tell him to be patient. Once in a while I'd get time off from my job and I'd go to see him."

"Those visits from Gus always helped to calm me down," Bill said. "I'd be real mad at myself, but Gus would straighten me out."

In 1958 Monbo was pitching for Minneapolis, which was then a Red Sox farm team. He had won only eight games while losing nine; but he had lost some of them by very close scores. One Sunday morning he was in his hotel room, getting ready to go to church, when the phone rang. It was the team's manager.

"You're going up to the Red Sox," he told Monbo.

"I thought it was a gag," Monbo said later. "I thought it was my roommate or one of the other guys horsing around, and I told him to cut it out. It must have taken the manager five minutes to convince me it was true."

Monbo finished that season with the Red Sox, winning four and losing three. His few starts convinced everybody that he was going to be a star.

"I guess the only day I really got nervous was when I found out my parents were coming to the ball park to see me pitch," he said. "Just thinking about my parents in the stands made me so nervous I could hardly stand up to go out there and warm up. But when the game started I was all right."

It took him a couple of years to learn how to pitch in the major leagues. But now somebody else besides Gus was teaching him—Sal Maglie!

Sal had retired as a player, and he had been hired by the Red Sox to coach their young pitchers. Once somebody asked Monbouquette how much he had been helped by Maglie.

"Plenty," Bill said. "He's a great pitching coach, and he keeps me on the ball, too. He hollers at me all the time when I'm out there pitching. He keeps after me so that I keep my mind on what I'm doing and concentrate on every pitch. He doesn't let me ease up and make the little mistakes that can cost the game. But afterwards he never says, 'Nice game.' He ignores me, and then I say to myself, 'I'll show that guy.' And the next time I try to do even better."

Monbo believes it is his ability to *concentrate*— to think about what he is doing and put all his skills behind each pitch—that made him a big league star.

"You can't afford to make any kind of mistake when you're pitching in the big leagues," Monbo says. "Especially when your team isn't getting you many runs. You've got to make every pitch count."

Bill also had to learn how to control his temper.

"I finally learned not to let my temper get the best of me like it used to," he told a sports writer during an interview. "I've always been nervous and excitable, I guess. I used to get mad when a guy hit a homer off me. When the other team used to holler at me from their dugout I'd blow my top. Now I know I was only hurting myself."

Bill held up his hand and pointed to his fingernails. "See," he said. "They're pretty good now. I used to bite my nails all the time. But I'm not as nervous as I was. I still have trouble sleeping after I pitch, but I don't worry much before a game."

In 1960, Bill almost pitched a no-hit game

Monbo pitches against the White Sox on August 1, 1962.

against the Tigers. They got only one hit. Later in
the season, he was given the honor of being the
starting pitcher for the American League in the
All-Star Game. In 1961 he got off to a poor start,
but Maglie worked with him and he improved.

By 1962, Monbo was an outstanding pitcher. In
his first start of the season, he pitched a 12-inning
shutout against the Indians. But, during the last
half of the season, the Red Sox' pitching staff fell
apart. No one was pitching well, and even Monbo
was having his troubles. He had pitched a complete game to beat Kansas City on June 29. Then,
throughout the whole month of July, neither Monbouquette nor anyone else on the staff pitched well
enough to stay on the mound for a whole game.

On August 1, Bill started against the White Sox
at Chicago. His opposing pitcher was Early Wynn,
one of the best of his time and still, at 42 years of
age, very tough to beat. The Red Sox got an occasional hit off Wynn, but could not score. Meanwhile, Monbouquette was cutting down the White
Sox' hitters. The only Chicago batter to reach base
was Al Smith, who walked in the second inning.

Monbo had thrown mostly curve balls and sliders
through the early innings of the game. "His slider
wasn't sharp in the early innings," said Jim Pagliaroni, who was catching for the Red Sox that day.
"We stopped using it, but in the fifth inning I called
for it again once or twice and suddenly I saw it was

sharp. So we stopped using the curve, and stayed with the slider and the fast ball."

The Red Sox finally scored in the top of the eighth inning. Pagliaroni singled and advanced to second base on a "blooper" hit by Pete Runnels. Then Lu Clinton, who had already singled twice off Wynn, got his third hit of the game, a sharp single to left field. Pagliaroni raced home and the Red Sox led, 1-0.

Monbo knew he had a no-hit game within his grasp, and he was determined not to lose it, as he had two years before against Detroit.

"When I started the eighth inning," Monbo said, "I told myself I would just have to break my back out there those last two innings."

In the eighth inning, he retired the White Sox without any trouble. Then he walked out to the mound to pitch the ninth. The first batter was Sherman Lollar, and Monbo never gave him a chance. He struck out the White Sox' big catcher on three pitches. Then Nelson Fox was sent up to pinch hit for Wynn.

"Fox was the batter I was really worried about," Monbo said later. "He always gets a piece of the ball."

But Monbo threw him a slider and Fox hit the ball on the ground to the third baseman for the second out. The last batter was Luis Aparicio. Luis fouled off two pitches in a row. Monbouquette

After pitching his no-hitter, Monbouquette endures the playful antics of catcher Jim Pagliaroni. Looking on at the left is Lu Clinton, whose single in the eighth inning drove in Pagliaroni for the Red Sox' only run.

pitched again, and Aparicio began to swing, then held back. Pagliaroni, thinking it was a third strike, leaped into the air for joy, but the umpire called it a ball. Keeping his temper, Monbo came right back with a slider and Aparicio swung at it and missed.

Bill Monbouquette had finally pitched his no-hitter. It was a proud day for him—and for Gus Hennessy, too!

10. One...Two... Three...Four!

Probably every boy, at some time or other, dreams of being able to throw a baseball as fast as Sandy Koufax. Knowing the story of Koufax, a boy might think that it would be wonderful to be signed to a contract for a great deal of money while he is still in his teens. He might also think how thrilling it would be to avoid spending even a day in the minor leagues and join a big league team that is on its way to a world championship.

This was the way Sandy Koufax' major league career began. He seemed to be on top of the world before he ever pitched an inning of professional baseball. However, it is wise to be skeptical of such success stories. Sandy Koufax would be the first to admit that nothing comes easy—even when a person has to start out at the top.

Unlike many great athletes, Sandy did not come from a poor home. His father was a lawyer, and lived in Brooklyn, New York. And, unlike many great pitchers, Sandy did not pitch a great deal while he went to school. He occasionally played first base, pitched a little, and was known as a basketball player when he entered college after high-school graduation.

But Sandy Koufax did not have to pitch very often to attract someone's attention. The Brooklyn Dodgers' scouts knew all about him. And when he was 19 years old they gave him a bonus to sign with the Dodgers.

In the spring of 1955, Sandy went right to the Dodgers' training camp. It seemed like a marvelous experience for a young man. In those days the Dodgers were a powerful team. But Sandy, like a lot of other hard-throwing young men, could not get the ball over the plate. To make matters worse, he hurt his back early in the season. When he was strong again, the Dodgers were fighting for the pennant and they didn't want to take a chance on an inexperienced pitcher.

So Sandy got very little chance to pitch that year. He thought that perhaps the next year would be different. But it wasn't. And neither was the next. The Dodgers were bringing up other young pitchers who had gained their experience in the minor leagues. In the few games that Sandy managed to start, he struck out a number of batters, but he walked a lot of them, too. Sandy Koufax was a big league pitcher. But he was not getting into many big league ball games.

At the end of six years with the Dodgers (who had moved to Los Angeles in 1958), Sandy's record was not much to brag about. During all those seasons, he had won only 36 games, and had lost 40. Yet all the time, Sandy was working hard to improve himself. He was learning how to get the ball over the plate. He was also learning how to throw a curve ball. After he developed a curve, many of the batters in the National League said it was even harder to hit than his fast ball.

Koufax did not become a winning pitcher until 1961. That season he won 18 games, and broke the modern National League record by striking out 269 batters. From then on, until he retired at the end of the 1966 season, Sandy Koufax was the most important player in baseball. When his arm was healthy, the Dodgers won the pennant. When he was hurt, the Dodgers slipped out of first place.

During the first half of 1962, Sandy was simply overpowering the National League batters. On June 30 of that year, he pitched his first no-hit game, beating the New York Mets, 5-0. It did not

Koufax is shown pitching during his no-hitter against the Mets. The scoreboard in the background shows a line of zeros for the Mets.

look as if any other team could stop the Dodgers. Then, in July, Koufax injured his left index-finger, which is so important to a left-handed pitcher in holding the ball. The injury impaired the blood circulation, causing the finger to go numb. Sandy could not pitch again that year, and the Dodgers, who were leading the league at the time, finally lost the pennant.

As 1963 began, many people wondered if Sandy would ever pitch in the big leagues again. But he came back stronger than ever. On May 11, he pitched a no-hit game against the Dodgers' old rivals, the Giants. It was the second no-hitter of his career. He went on to win 25 games and pitch the Dodgers to the pennant. Then, in the World Series, he beat the Yankees twice, and the Dodgers won in four straight games.

In 1964, Sandy again appeared to be the best pitcher in baseball. On June 4, for the third year in a row, he pitched a no-hit game to beat the Phillies, 3-0. Then, once again, an injury put him out of action for the rest of the season, and the Dodgers dropped out of the pennant race.

When Sandy returned to the Dodgers in 1965, he knew that his big league career could end at any time. He suffered from arthritis in his left elbow, which made it extremely painful for him to pitch. In spite of his handicap, he had already established himself as one of the great fast-ball pitchers of all

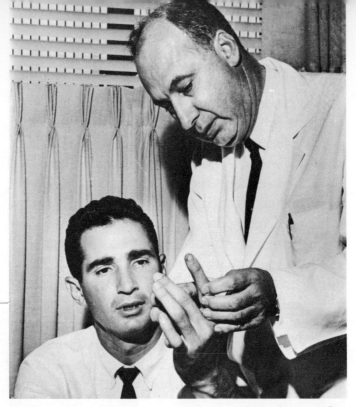

Dr. Robert Wood examines Sandy's left index finger, which was numbed by impaired blood circulation.

time. Twice he had tied Bob Feller's record by striking out 18 batters in a game.

The Dodgers of 1965 were one of the weakest hitting teams anyone in baseball could remember. They seldom supported their pitchers by scoring runs.

"I try to pitch a shutout every time," Koufax said. "One run is all I can count on from our team."

But the Dodgers had an outstanding pitching staff. In addition to Koufax, Don Drysdale and

Claude Osteen helped to keep the team in the pennant race. As the season entered its final weeks, the Dodgers battled the Giants for the pennant, and Koufax crept closer to Bob Feller's modern record of 343 strikeouts in a season.

"I'm not trying to strike out every hitter," Sandy said. "The only time I really try for strikeouts is when there's a runner on third base who can hurt me by scoring. Otherwise, I prefer to get the batter out on a fly ball or a grounder. I throw fewer pitches that way and save wear and tear on my arm."

In September, it began to look as if not even Koufax could keep the Dodgers in the pennant race. They did not have a man in the line-up whose batting average even approached .300. No one had hit as many as ten home runs. And their best pinch hitter was Don Drysdale—a pitcher!

Then, on September 9, with the Dodgers fighting to get out of a slump, they played the Chicago Cubs at Los Angeles. Walter Alston, the Dodgers' manager, named Koufax to pitch against the Cubs' young left-hander, Bob Hendley. Inning after inning, Sandy mowed down the Cubs' hitters. But the Dodgers' hitters were so ineffective that they made Hendley look as good as Koufax. After four innings no batter on either side had even reached first base. The Dodgers finally scored in the fifth inning.

Outfielder Lou Johnson walked, and was pushed

to second by a sacrifice bunt. Then he took a big lead off the base. When Hendley pitched to the plate, Johnson started to steal third. The Cubs' catcher fired the ball wildly past third base into left field. Johnson kept right on running and came in to score the run that put the Dodgers ahead, 1-0. As usual, this was about the only way the Dodgers were able to score.

In the seventh inning, Johnson came up again and doubled, but he did not get any farther. Hendley did not allow another Dodger batter to reach base in the game.

Unfortunately, Hendley was up against baseball's best pitcher, who was pitching the finest game of his career. After seven innings, the Cubs still had not gotten a runner to first base by *any* means.

Ron Santo, the Cubs' hard-hitting third baseman, led off against Koufax in the eighth inning. Koufax put two strikes over the plate, then came back with a curve ball which Santo took for a called third strike. Ernie Banks, one of the most dangerous hitters in the league, was the next batter. Koufax was throwing hard now, and Banks never had a chance. Sandy struck him out. Then he finished the inning by striking out Byron Browne.

The Cubs had one more chance to stop Koufax. When Sandy went out to defend his 1-0 lead and his perfect game in the ninth inning, he was greeted

by a howling, excited mob. He went right to work
on Chris Krug and struck him out. Joe Amalfitano
came up as a pinch hitter. Sandy was blazing fast
now. He threw three straight strikes past the helpless Cub batter, and now there were two out.

The Cubs sent up Harvey Kuenn, a former batting champion, to pinch-hit for Hendley. Koufax
knew he would have to put something extra on the
ball if he was going to throw it past Kuenn, and he
did. Mixing his fast balls and curves, he ran the

Koufax receives a sign from his catcher.

count on Kuenn to two-and-two. Then Koufax made his next pitch a fast ball, and Kuenn watched it go by for strike three!

The strikeout, Sandy's fourteenth of the game, was one of the most important of his career. It gave the Dodgers an important victory in the pennant race. It also gave Sandy his *fourth* no-hit game, a record which no other pitcher in the history of baseball has matched. And, finally, it meant that Koufax had pitched one of the seven *perfect* games in the major leagues during this century.

Bob Hendley had allowed just one hit and one walk, but that was enough to beat him. Throughout the history of the major leagues, it has often happened that the man who pitched a no-hit game defeated a man who pitched almost as well.

Sandy did not rest after that game, no matter how important it had been. In his next two starts, he had to be almost as good, for he won both games by the same score, 1-0. On September 25, he struck out 12 St. Louis batters and broke Bob Feller's record. He went on to set a new record of 382 strikeouts for the season. On the next to the last day of the pennant race, he beat the Braves, 3-1, to clinch the flag for the Dodgers.

When Sandy's arthritic elbow finally forced him to retire a year later, there were many records he could look back on with pride. His victory totals, his World Series achievements and his strikeout

*In the last few innings of Sandy's famous game
against the Cubs, he was throwing hard. Here, the
force of his pitch has caused him to lose his cap.*

Koufax is mobbed by his teammates after pitching a perfect game against the Cubs.

records will be remembered for a long time. But perhaps none of his records will last as long or shine as brightly as those four no-hit games—the last of them a perfect game at a time when his team needed it the most. This is a record that could have been made only by a *great* pitcher.

Index

Page numbers in italics refer to photographs

About the Author

Frank Graham, Jr. has been involved in baseball most of his life. The son of a popular sports writer, he has been the publicity director for the old Brooklyn Dodgers, an editor with *Sport* Magazine, and is a regular contributor to *Sports Illustrated*. He is also the author of a number of books, including a biography of Casey Stengel and *Great Pennant Races of the Major Leagues* (Little League Library #7). He and his wife live in Milbridge, Maine.